So This Is How It Feels to Be a Wife

Insightful Guidance for the Long Haul

• Terri L. Smith •

To the rosebuds that keep my heart beating,
Tori and Ana.

The women here can teach beyond my capacity.
Make their wisdom your own.

May your garden bloom all the days of your life.

Love forever,

Mommy

xoxox

Table of Contents

Acknowledgements

I want to thank all of the fabulous women who participated in this project. Of course, this includes almost all the women I have ever known. I am especially grateful to those women who were willing to be interviewed for this project. I appreciate your significant time commitment to the project and your willingness to share very personal situations, feelings, failures, and successes. It is my wish that this book reflect each of you and your marriages accurately and in a way that makes you proud. You should be.

It is also my wish that the readers of this book benefit from your generosity and your insight. I know I certainly did. You have enriched my life beyond belief, and I am enormously grateful.

I also want to thank my daughters who tolerate me every day, some days more pleasantly than others, but you tolerate me nonetheless. I know this project represented a huge change in our daily lives and that some days you would have preferred me to be a working stiff, trotting off to a remote office somewhere far, far away. Please accept my apologies for *being in your face* too often. May what you glean from this book be well worth the long days and hard nights. I love you even more than I love Harry. (And that is saying a whole lot! He remains, however, the cutest thing on this planet.)

As for my next husband, wherever you might be, I thank you for not arriving yet. I look like hell when I am writing.

To my sister, Dolores Queen, God bless you and your family, especially that husband of yours. You are the steadfast glue that keeps me together when all around me goes haywire.

To my dearest friends, Rochelle Massarella, Pat Burns, Dene Harris, Paula Jones, Diane Gobeil, Pat Mummert, Robbie Galati, Adrienne Mendel, Barbara Sicalides, Marc Klebanoff, and Jay Gee, my time with you is always valued more than you may know.

Thank you for all your support no matter how crazy a situation I might find myself. Italy next summer?

I also want to thank some very special women I know whose help and guidance were enormously instrumental in putting this book together namely Amy Pooser, Betty Hirsch, Tracey Huddleston, Leslie Heffernen, Dana Heiman, Colleen Marzella, Nicole Dressel, Carol Alesi, Paula and Samantha Soprano, Estelle Supreme, and Francine Carb.

To Mark Victor Hansen and Mary Langford. Good God! You two arrived in my life right on time! Thank you for the structure you provided and your effervescent and unending encouragement and enthusiasm. Without you, this book would never be in print.

I am very proud of myself for not being sappy with these acknowledgements. I have become so mature. Miracles happen every day!

Love,

Terri

P.S. To those I didn't mention, like Tommy and Dorothy, you are in my heart and soul, every day. We will see each other again. xoxo

Preface
Why Write This?

You might be asking what in the name of God prompted me to write a book about wives in marriages that function well. The answer is easy—I am not one, so there is a natural curiosity.

And suddenly life gave me some extra time to devote to the project. The economy left me happily unemployed from a lengthy and stressful career in financial services; my long-term relationship was unexpectedly terminated and, if you ask me, terminated in its prime. As you can imagine, there isn't an abundance of open positions in financial services, new significant others can't be ordered on the Internet for next-day delivery, and my two teenage daughters were in school during the day. I needed something to fill the time besides surfing the net, cleaning out the garage, closing my E-Harmony matches, and expanding my LinkedIn connections.

Therefore, I decided to put my time to good use. I thought my most recent relationship had many of the ingredients for a long-term success, but when my best bud placed my house key under my front door mat with the intention of never using it again, it was clear that only I felt that way. I guess I really wanted to find out where I went wrong and what exactly was lacking in this relationship. I decided that talking to women about their marriages could help solve the mystery. What I discovered is going to be of no great revelation to those in successful relationships. It appears that there are common ingredients to make a marriage work. BUT to those of us without these ingredients, the results are revealing and yet largely common sense, as you will see.

I interviewed women whose marriages were only a few months old to women who were well past celebrating their six-tieth wedding anniversary. I interviewed women who have been married only once, and women who have been married, not once, not twice, but three times. (Thankfully, I did not find a third marriage that wasn't working! It appears that usually by number three, these women have a good sense of the necessary ingredients.)

Some women were wonderfully candid and revealing, and others were reluctant to have anyone link them to their commentary and spoke only on condition of anonymity. I interviewed widows whose husbands lived on so vividly in their hearts and souls, that I had a strong sense of their loss decades after his death. I interviewed women who had no wifely role model as a child, and women who had many. All the women I interviewed are amazing.

For those of you who want the reward of a fulfilling, time-tested, and sustainable marriage, this book is for you. The gems I found in homes throughout America are something you can create behind your own front door. Take the plunge and read on. You have nothing to lose and much to gain.

*Some roses
are so strong that they bloom reliably
despite adverse conditions.*

Chapter • One

Sarah

Born on October 10, 1930, Sarah grew up in the Germantown and Mount Airy sections of Philadelphia. Not only did she have a mother, father, and one younger brother, but her maternal grandmother, a vibrant role model for Sarah, lived with them for many years.

Some women worked outside the home when Sarah was a child, but there were very few professional opportunities and one of the few was teaching. Regardless of whether or not the wives worked, they were homemakers. Sarah summed it up this way, "Most of the men ran the money and did nothing around the house."

Sarah's grandmother was born in Texas to a family of means. She met her husband in Cincinnati. They married, and a few years after their marriage, her husband's business failed. At the age of forty-eight, she moved with her husband to Philly. At that point their children were eleven and twelve. Her young husband passed away unexpectedly when the children were still dependents. After he died, Sarah's grandmother had to go to work to support herself and her children. She landed an interesting job as a comparison shopper for a downtown department store. She would spend time in competitors' stores and report back to her employer on items and pricing of their competitors.

Like her own mother before her, Sarah's mother worked. She began teaching sixth grade boys when she was only eighteen. She married at age twenty-two and taught until she had her first child, Sarah, two years later.

Sarah readily states, "I have to say that my mother was one of the brightest women I have ever known." Dad was a traveling salesman and not home much. Mom was "in charge" and worked hard.

She cared for her two children, took care of her ailing mother, and was a fabulous cook and a good homemaker. After Sarah's brother, Eddie, started junior high, their mother returned to teaching.

Sarah's memory serves her mother well; she sees her mom as a strong, independent, capable woman who had many close women friends. All are traits that Sarah's life also embraces.

Sarah's mother worked until two months before her death of leukemia at the age of sixty. Her mother, like Shirley Temple Black, was one of the first people to speak openly about her cancer. "She left us all heartbroken, and at the age of thirty-five, I became the matriarch."

Sarah recounts her childhood years with gratitude and joy. "I was very lucky. I went to Logan Demonstration School. I had to be tested. It was a demonstration school for other teachers. There were always other teachers observing in the back of the room."

During this time a family might have one car but not two or more. The neighborhood parents joined forces to send their young children to school in a cab. But by the time Sarah was in third grade, she was taking public transportation alone.

She went on to Girls High, and subsequently went to the University of Pennsylvania on a full scholarship. "It was a fluke. I still don't know where that came from. I had to study elementary education. I was at Penn, and went three and a half years."

From the time Sarah was a little girl, she wanted to be married, and never considered any other life. She was twelve when she had her first boyfriend; she dated many guys but didn't have a serious relationship until she met her husband, Danny. She was nineteen and he was twenty-four. After a couple of dates, Sarah was certain that she wanted Danny as her husband. But it took Danny two and a half years to propose.

At twenty-one, Sarah started teaching in a "fancy school in Chestnut Hill," but she was driven to have a greater effect on the world. To Sarah, this meant becoming a teacher in the Philadelphia school system, a position she held until her marriage.

Later that year, she married Danny and began working for the Friends Service Committee, a position she thoroughly enjoyed. Shortly thereafter, she had her first daughter, Casey, and Sarah stopped working. Exactly like her mother, Sarah married at age twenty-two and had her first child at age twenty-four.

Later, with her children in school, and her husband established in a new career, Sarah volunteered with a children's agency and, at age fifty, this evolved into a paid part-time position that she held until she was sixty-three. Today she draws on her love of art and of children as she volunteers leading art appreciation classes in local schools.

Her expectations of the marriage included knowing that there would be difficulties to overcome together. She realized that "We might disagree, but we would work it out." She was in for the long haul. For Sarah and Danny, thoughts of divorce were taboo. Under no conceivable circumstance would they ever accept divorce as a viable alternative regardless of the severity of their tough times. The problems they had were their *joint* problems, and the shared value that their family always comes first is fundamental to their relationship.

Sarah's childhood fairy tale, like most young girls' of her day, was that you fall madly in love, and you are able to solve all problems as a team. In order to make that happen, however, Sarah will tell you that the most important thing in a marriage is to talk—not always on THAT day, but you need to talk. "There will never be any two people who won't argue, BUT you have to talk about it. Danny didn't like to talk." But Danny was very willing and able to provide the emotional support that Sarah so desperately needed when trouble set in.

Danny and Sarah happily planned to have three or four children. But in less than five years, Sarah had five pregnancies, three heart-wrenching miscarriages, and an unwelcome surgery. They talked about adopting.

To both Sarah and Danny, this period of time was one of the most stressful periods of their marriage. Sarah was driven to make it work and said, "I was going to DO THIS." The toll on her was both emotionally and physically demanding. Danny was enormously supportive during this extended trial, but as a young husband, he was learning daily how to be supportive and how to communicate.

"I was always a social person...wanted to talk things out. My parents always argued, but I was always aware that my mother was a major communicator who could 'soften the blow' of the arguments."

"When Casey was born, my doctor induced, and my parents were excited for their first grandchild. They sat in one waiting room, and Danny sat in another. Danny is a 'loner type of person.' However, as time went on, he became more supportive and warmer to my parents. We all grow."

The next trial came after the successful pregnancy and birth of their second daughter, Gail, and around the time of Sarah's surgery. Danny's father had a good business where Danny was employed, but it was liquidated when Danny was thirty-five. Sarah and Danny had never expected the financial problems that resulted.

Sarah saw their financial hardship as her chance to support him after all the wonderful support he had provided to her during the period of her miscarriages. "I always had faith. He is bright and skilled, and it never entered my head that he would not land on his feet." Sarah also never lost her sense of appreciation for what she had. "We lived simply during those lousy years, but I was never forced to go to work, which was really nice for me."

Sarah very clearly remembers being in the hospital after surgery. Her roommate was a woman with eight children whose husband rarely came to visit. In contrast and like clockwork, Danny came to visit every afternoon during visiting hours. Sarah's roommate said to her one day, "You are so lucky you have a Jewish husband. He comes to see you every afternoon!" Sarah didn't have the heart to tell her that Danny wasn't working and had "nothing better to do."

Today, in their seventies and eighties, their biggest challenges come in the form of Sarah's numerous physical problems. For Sarah not only does Danny give emotional support, but today with Sarah's painful illness she also says, "Many of my husband's generation are much more helpful than the generation before. He gives wonderful physical support."

Their main focus continues to be their own relationship, and their relationship with their daughters and their daughters' families. They see their children regularly and vacation with them at least once a year. Sarah is very grateful to both Casey and Gail for how inclusive they are, always making time for conversation and dinner with their parents.

Together not only do they enjoy time with their children and grandchildren but also they make special time for the two of them alone. "We both love travel, and we have enjoyed many trips alone and with other people."

Sarah attributes the longevity of their marriage to respect, mutual support, shared core values, and having very separate and distinct interests from one another. Sarah says, "Danny likes tennis, and I like swimming. Danny likes computers, and I like bridge. Danny likes music, and I love art." In fact, Sarah is a prolific and talented painter mostly of still lifes and landscapes.

By having different interests, they have activities away from one another that allow them to interact with others and stay young. It also gives them something to talk about when they are together.

Sarah wants to paint your beautiful rose garden when it is enriched by the following ways:

1. Relationships with others are very important. Maintain and foster strong friendships.
2. Look for and acknowledge to your spouse the good things you see. This is especially important during the tough times but should be done during good times as well.
3. Provide support and accept support. Make your home one where you each support one another. A good marriage needs mutual emotional support, and for this, you have to have good communication skills.
4. Insist on talking through problems, but see yourself as a peacemaker. Live the role of a peacemaker.
5. When an issue is not of paramount importance, have the ability to give in. "This is very important. You don't want to kill each other over nothing."
6. Make sure you can say, "I am sorry. I was wrong."
7. Always have a sense of humor.
8. Don't dwell on a problem. In the words of Sarah's mother, "Don't wear your dirty laundry on your sleeve." In other words, don't become one of your moaning, complaining married friends. We all have a couple of them! (If you ask me, many of them really do have something to complain about!)
9. Always maintain a good attitude and have the right expectations for your marriage. Expect your marriage to be good and then work to make it good. If your gut is telling you not to marry or that things aren't right, listen to what your gut is telling you.
10. No matter what, make time for vacations, preferably a trip to experience new things together. This is a great way to refresh your relationship.
11. Develop interests that are separate and distinct from your spouse's interests.

Propagating a beautiful new rosebush
from a strong existing bush
is easy to do.

Chapter • Two

Gail, Sarah's Daughter

Gail's childhood was stressful given that her sister was five years her senior, and they argued as intensely as any good sisters do. (Fortunately, they are all grown up now and thoroughly enjoy each other's company!) Despite the squabbles with her sister, Gail remembers a wonderful sense of stability in her childhood home—stability derived from the mutual respect, equality, individuality, and love between her parents.

Gail's only real role model of how a wife should be was her mother, who will celebrate her fifty-eighth wedding anniversary this year. Clearly Gail's parents illustrate just how long a loving marriage can last.

Gail unequivocally stated that her parents have had a traditional marriage, but she quickly added, "Traditional but not subservient—an equal partnership." She further added that while she would consider their marriage traditional, for instance, her mom didn't work until Gail was older, neither parent treated each other in traditional ways.

Her mom was not a strident feminist but a strong woman with a firm and immutable sense of her own identity. She didn't need her husband's approval. She was liberal politically. She was never subservient and did not spend her days making sure father was happy. She was active in volunteer efforts but resumed working when her girls were older.

Gail's parents rarely fought. They had a homogenous view of the world, and believed that family always comes first and that married people, especially married people with kids, stayed married. In fact, most of the parents in the neighborhood shared this same view except for the one divorcee whose husband left her and about whom the entire neighborhood talked quite openly.

One of her childhood friends had an atypically liberal mother. She let her kids get high in the house. This mother was really unusual in terms of what she did and didn't do. As a young girl, Gail "thought she was really cool."

Observing her parents' seemingly happy, longstanding marriage had a wonderfully positive impact. She saw that her parents have a lot of respect for each other. Early on through her childhood eyes, she saw what a well-functioning, supportive marriage looks like. She also realized that marriage wasn't quite what you saw on TV, but it was expected that "you got married when you were young and had a couple of kids." For Gail this vision of her future didn't require much analysis. Marriage was "a given" in Gail's childhood world, although today Gail would tell you that as a young woman she was never certain that marriage was in her future.

Gail married Stephen when she was twenty-eight. "I knew we were very compatible. We wanted the same things, and we had a good time together. I could not think of what was ahead, but I was ready. It was the same as when the baby was coming. I knew I wanted to be married and have kids." Gail is also equally certain that "I didn't marry Stephen because I wanted to be married. I married Stephen because I wanted to be with him." Their first of two children arrived four years later.

Communication has been an ongoing workshop for Gail and Stephen. (Are we reading about Gail's marriage or Sarah's marriage?) They react to the world differently. For one thing, Gail is much more emotional and expressive than her husband. He tends to be laid back and happily passive.

If he has a problem or doesn't like something, Stephen withdraws into himself. "It takes a little work to draw him out and that is frustrating to me...It has evolved with him. He wants to be drawn out, but I want to saw him in half sometimes." (I see what Gail means when she says she is more expressive!) And she adds lightheartedly with a smile on her face, "Put twenty-five of him in the room, I would be the only one talking!"

Gail and one of her closest girlfriends joke about their fights with their husbands. "The fights we have with our husbands are the *same three fights*. I know what is going to be said, and I know it isn't even worth the fight. Have it and get all bent out of shape about it? Here is my practicality coming through. I am much more emotional and expressive, so in order for us to have a fight I really have to pull it out of him. He really doesn't want to have a fight... and I think that is a good thing."

Any frustrations that Gail has with the day-to-day life of the marriage are not long lasting or permanent or scarring. Sometimes she confronts straight on what she doesn't like in their relationship, and "sometimes I just get over it or I might whine about it."

But not all of life's challenges are just little irritants that can be washed away with a whine and a concerted change in attitude. Some situations are stressful and last more than a day, a week, or a month.

Heartbreak and stress came to them in the form of infertility. Because of their joint desire for children, they began the arduous task of artificial insemination. When Gail talks of the experience, she can recall the pain, the worry, and the upset. She remembers asking herself over and over again what was wrong with her that she couldn't get pregnant.

After four or five unfruitful (forgive the pun) inseminations, Gail became pregnant and gave birth to a beautiful baby boy. A couple of years later, they tried the process again, but the ending was not so sweet. Gail had a miscarriage. They loved their son so much, and they continued to be encouraged by their success with that pregnancy. So round three commenced, and this time Gail delivered a beautiful baby girl!

Today Gail rarely thinks about the pain of those years. The joy of her children and their life as a family has supplanted the difficulty of the children's arrivals. I guess it is similar to a mother's ability to forget the pain of labor as soon as the baby is delivered—the joy far outweighs the pain.

AND in Gail's usual style she can find some humor in any situation. She recounts with bittersweet laughter the memory of anxious parents filling the doctor's waiting room and holding seemingly fragile sperm containers, kept cozy in socks.

Problems rarely come just once in a marriage, and Gail and Stephen were no exception. "We have had periods of un- and underemployment...I never felt like we were going to lose our house, and I didn't ever want to blame Stephen. There were times I blamed him, but it was never his fault. And I resented him, but I knew I wasn't being rational. Stephen wanted to work."

Gail is quick to emphasize that in the early days of their marriage when they both worked full time, Stephen shot ahead of her in earnings. Since the birth of their children, Gail has only worked part time. Her main contribution has been caring for the children.

During the most challenging times, Gail tapped into her known strengths. Gail, like other women in her lineage, is a strong communicator. She is persistent, patient, enormously competent, reliable, and supportive. Friends and family have always been a big source of support.

Like her mother, Gail would not consider herself spiritual and has never sought comfort or support from her religion. In fact, religion could have been a conflict in their marriage. Gail is Jewish and Stephen is Catholic. Early in their relationship, they acknowledged their differences and moved on. "We celebrate the holidays of both our traditions" and don't emphasize either religion in the raising of their son and daughter.

The most fulfilling times of their marriage revolve around parenting together. To Gail and Stephen, each child's accomplishments are a reflection of their joint parenting. It is a joy they can share and talk about.

Today Stephen's job necessitates travel. Consequently, in the day-to-day issues, Gail takes the lead with the children. In regard to Stephen's heavy travel schedule, "I am not sure that this is always a bad thing. BUT there are times when it is awful."

"Generally in raising the kids, I always think that I am right and he agrees, but when we have a difference of opinion, I will absolutely listen to what he has to say. Since he generally doesn't disagree with me, I have to listen and do things his way unless I really disagree."

Stephen clearly has a respect for Gail's parenting skills. He doesn't feel he needs to know everything about every day. But Gail is adamant that parenting is a shared responsibility. "We always talk about the important things."

Gail and I are sitting in a coffee shop talking about the good Stephen brings to the family. While we chat, Stephen is making plans for a three-day trip for him with just their daughter to celebrate her fourteenth birthday. Gail is ecstatic about it. She loves the way Stephen loves their children, and she loves the ways he expresses it to them. "Stephen is a very good presence in their lives and that is another thing I really love about him."

Gail has been married over twenty years. Her advice for your garden is straightforward and sound.

1. Don't expect your marriage to be all passion and attraction. It is work to create a marriage in which both people are happy and thrive.

2. Give yourself a reality check. Falling in love, planning the wedding, and newlywed life is not the real world. It is not what your marriage really is. "**That** is the really good stuff that happens when the relationship is new. You have to think beyond that to a little bit more of the day to day, month to month, and year to year. You know, like when the guy gets hair growing out of his ears..."

3. Although Gail didn't articulate it to me, she certainly embodies what her mother already advised—have a sense of humor! Little trials or irritations can be perfectly soothed by a little laughter. Laugh at yourself and laugh together—daily.

4. Take time to notice and to appreciate the good your spouse brings to the relationship and to the family. Make sure he knows how you feel.

Your job, should you choose to accept it, is to identify all the similarities and the differences between Gail and her marriage and her mother, Sarah, and her marriage.

When you prune, which you must do,
you must cut the stems
that are crisscrossing, touching, or
otherwise encroaching on one another.

Chapter • Three

Leslie

Leslie was born in 1969 in Syracuse, New York, the youngest of three. Her parents are still married, and she comes from a close-knit extended family. Her paternal grandparents lived down the street during her childhood.

Leslie's biological paternal grandfather passed away when he was a young husband. Leslie never knew him. With a bit of serendipity, Leslie's grandmother reunited with a childhood friend whose spouse had also passed away. They each had been single about ten years. "He wrote her a letter asking for a proper date. He had dated her older sister when they were kids. She was a pest. She spied on them because she liked him." In 1970, at ages seventy and seventy-five, they married. Leslie was only one-year-old at the time, and always thought of him as her true grandfather. Her grandparents adored one other, and openly displayed their affection by holding hands. Her grandfather was enormously handsome and hardworking. He did not retire from their farm until the age of ninety-eight.

Leslie vividly recalls when her grandfather was hospitalized for a knee replacement. By this time, Leslie was old enough to drive, and she drove her grandmother to the hospital to visit him. Her grandmother had been anxiously awaiting the visit and was ready hours before Leslie's arrival. Leslie recalls, "She was waiting with her purse on her lap and her sweater on." When they arrived at the hospital, her grandfather grabbed his wife and pulled her up onto the bed with him. "He was about ninety-six at the time, and very loving."

Leslie fondly remembers her grandmother. "She was a good farmer's wife…She would cook and clean while he would be out working in the barn. They ate every meal together. They had a routine."

Her grandparents' open affection led young Leslie to believe that when you are married you can be very affectionate. Leslie's own parents, however, were "together all the time, and were close but not affectionate." Leslie's impression of her parents is that they have always been more like friends. Her grandparents were more like "kids in love." Both couples were always respectful toward each, and there was never any fighting.

Leslie's grandparents strongly influenced what she wanted for herself in a marriage. "I wanted an affectionate husband like my grandfather...I wanted that cutesiness, that fun stuff. She [her grandmother] would be openly jealous. My grandmother would make faces behind the nurses' back. I liked that. I thought it was funny."

Both of Leslie's parents had full-time jobs, and they drove to work together every day. Her mom was a social worker with the county for twenty-five years and was in charge of the house. Dad had a thirty-year career with Travelers Insurance. Like Leslie's grandparents, they, too, had their set routine.

Leslie sees both her mom and her dad as strong individuals who have never been needy. She cannot recall ever seeing either one upset. If there ever were upsetting issues, they were handled out of the children's sight and hearing. Leslie's childhood home, with one older sister and one older brother, was the picture of suburban stability; because of her upbringing in a traditional home, Leslie identified strongly with the milestones of a traditional life. You go to college, date for a year or so, get married, and have kids. "The wife is primarily responsible for house and the kids, while the man should take care of cars and shoveling snow."

Her mother also raised her not to expect a fairy tale ending. Her mother grew up in Colombia, South America, and left as a young adult to escape machismo. "Mom wanted nothing to do with that...she left....to marry someone who respected her." Leslie's mom raised Leslie to expect a lot more from a marriage as well.

For those of you not familiar with machismo, I will explain it to you the way Leslie learned it from her South American relatives. A man gets married, but he also has a girlfriend on the side. Commonly the wife and the mistress know about each other and accept this way of life. In fact, Leslie's aunt in Bogota was married to a man who impregnated his mistress multiple times. Each time, the husband would bring the child home to his wife for her to parent.

Leslie remembers being totally cognizant of this machismo as a child. Her mother would tell stories. At eight-years-old, when Leslie first went to Colombia and met her aunt's kids, "I knew they weren't my cousins. You have to be bitter."

She also clearly remembers meeting a fifteen-year-old girl who was married to a man about fifty-years-old. He would drive to visit his mistress and leave his child-wife in the car to wait until he was finished. At some point, the husband and wife would include sons on this type of visit. It was considered the son's "rite of passage."

Leslie was twenty-six when she met her husband in law school. "We were in class, and he said to his buddy who was sitting next to him, 'I am going to marry *that* girl.'" Nine months later they married. "We decided to get married in late August. School was starting, and we got married three weeks later. We had lived together for a month. He was the only guy I dated who wasn't a show-off...We were friends first."

She remembers having a "rotten boyfriend" in college. "He was so hotheaded. He saw me talking with another guy, and he flew off the handle and I was so embarrassed that I knew I didn't want anyone like that. It was obvious he didn't respect me. I was young, but I would have married that guy. I was stupid. He sucked the self-esteem out of me. If I hadn't been in college, I would have married him. So I see how people let this happen. They don't know any better. But going through this helped me to see the difference between guys."

Steve was raised Protestant, and Leslie was raised Catholic, but the Catholic Church wouldn't marry them because they would not do the Pre-Cana course that the church requires all couples to complete before marriage. The course usually runs approximately six weeks, and since they didn't want a long engagement, Leslie and Steve decided not to be married in the church. However, their children are being raised Catholic, although neither Leslie nor Steve would say religion is a driving force in their family. "It is not a focus or big part of our lives."

Leslie talked about other considerations that shaped their marriage plans. "We were realistic. We were both in school. We needed to save, and we didn't want to waste money on a big wedding."

At first, Leslie kept her finances separate, so it would be easier to walk away if the marriage didn't work out. But she feels she had a "reasonable expectation" that the marriage would work. "I would not risk everything on this one marriage. Plenty of people get married, and it doesn't work out." She didn't change her last name when they married, although she eventually did; she kept her money separate for about a year. On important issues, such as having children, they knew they were in agreement. "We knew that we both wanted kids."

In the early years of their marriage, they would visualize their future together. They lived in a suburban town, and they would take drives through their community and the surrounding area. They looked at homes on these rides and would say, "Someday we will have a house like that. We knew we would have a stable income, a house, and a few kids." After Leslie completed law school and a few years after their wedding day, they had the first of two beautiful daughters.

I asked Leslie if she could identify the most fulfilling time in her marriage. She didn't hesitate for a second before saying, "It should be when my kids were born, but it isn't. I think it was when I was pregnant with my first child. It was exciting, trying to do everything we could before the baby was born. We spent a lot of time together. We traveled a lot, worked on the baby's room…" Together they spent meaningful time in the wonderful anticipation of their first child.

Steve has always been respectful and flexible when Leslie expresses any want. "If I told him I wanted to quit my job and become a hairdresser, he would say, 'Okay. Whatever you want.'" Leslie finds Steve to be very supportive and easygoing.

Some of their most challenging times were when Steve's employer needed him in other locations. The first time Steve was needed in the Washington, DC office for a two-year commitment. Leslie and the girls planned to go with him. They were down to the last couple of weeks before their relocation, when Leslie told Steve that she couldn't possibly go. She liked her job, and she was afraid there would be nothing at all to come back to professionally in two years. It would be like starting her law practice all over again. Also, Leslie's parents had moved from out of state to be close to them when the first child arrived. "Just the thought of taking the kids from them—I couldn't do it."

At first, Steve was understandably upset. Yet, true to form, Steve remained flexible and respectful of Leslie's desires. He orchestrated an arrangement that allowed them to keep their house in suburban Philadelphia and get a second house in Maryland.

"We loved Maryland and DC, but I could not leave. He would come up for the weekend and every Sunday when he had to leave I would be so sad. The kids were little. The oldest was in preschool. We made it work. We had no choice, and eventually I got used to it and liked being on my own. I couldn't complain too much because it was a big deal for Steve to figure out the two places. We saw each other every weekend."

After Steve made the weekend commute from DC for a year, Leslie realized that she could not manage both caring for the girls and working for a demanding law firm. "It was too much. So I left to work with my father-in-law's firm." Leslie was able to have more control of her hours when partnering with her father-in-law.

After DC came the year-long assignment in the company's Manhattan office. Steve made the same dual home arrangements. Leslie and the girls enjoyed going to New York frequently on the weekends, and Steve came home on the other weekends.

Today, Steve is living at home, but Leslie really enjoys running the household and making all decisions on decorating and landscaping. She controls everything in the house just as her traditional upbringing encouraged. "I control everything in the house. My dad would plant flowers. Steve would never do that. I could hire someone to redo our entire yard, and Steve would not notice. He doesn't care how much I would spend. I like that. It gives me independence to do what I want, and he trusts me that I won't go blow all the money." When I commented that Steve must like her tastes, she responded that "he just doesn't notice." As for the children, they are largely Leslie's day-to-day responsibilities. "He will go to some kids' functions in the evening, but it is mostly me. He will work with them on weekends with sports stuff."

Even though Leslie is a well-respected attorney now in a solo practice (her father-in-law retired), Steve is largely responsible for the family's earnings. "He works, and he worries about what goes on in the office, and I worry about everything else. He is the breadwinner. If he lost his job, it would be different than if I lost mine."

Leslie says that she and Steve have their own rules. "He handles his job, which covers the important things like insurance. Although I work, I take care of stuff like getting the kids to school, camp, doctors' appointments, and the house. It works. We aren't on top of each other."

And just like Leslie's beloved grandparents, "we try to be 'cute' and have fun with one another." Leslie will send him funny e-mails that claim they are from "the ball and chain" or "the hag," and he does something similar in return. "If I want more affection, I just have to give more affection, and he will reciprocate."

Their marriage is one of respect, and each spouse pursues the friendships, interests, education, and the professional activities that each wants. And neither one is possessive.

Leslie has very specific beliefs regarding the reasons behind their strong marriage. "We respect each other, and we trust each other. I know he has to entertain clients. He will go to sports events on his own, and I trust that is what he is doing." Leslie laughs and adds jokingly, "But I am not stupid. I **do** look in his pockets!"

Leslie's father had bypass surgery about six years ago. "I was a mess, and I knew I could not go to the hospital." In this time of crisis, Steve had his turn at the controls. He handled getting his father-in-law's pre-op preparation. He took his in-laws to the hospital for the surgery, and he stayed with Leslie's mom all throughout the surgery. Leslie showed up much later, when the worst of the waiting was over.

"There was no way I could have done it. [Dad] probably weighed ninety pounds with triple bypass, a defective heart. He had been in bad shape for years and wasn't strong enough for surgery. I didn't even have to ask Steve. He just knew."

To Leslie, one of the more poignant moments in their relationship was when Steve had eye surgery last year. Leslie took him to the hospital and waited while he was in surgery. "It wasn't serious, but it could have been if the surgery went askew." When she recalls his being in a wheelchair and needing her help physically, she has a sense of how quickly things could change. Steve's eye surgery left her with a sense of appreciation of their life and of vulnerability because that good life can change any moment.

That time waiting in the hospital gave Leslie an opportunity to reflect on how wonderful her husband has been to her and her family.

Together they happily celebrated the fourteenth anniversary last September.

Leslie's gardening advice to wives:

1. You need to like each other.

    Trust your instincts; if you sense telltale signs that he might not be the perfect fit for you, he probably isn't. In Leslie's case, her instincts were shouting at her to avoid possessive, verbally abusive men. That is a good idea for all of us.

2. Always be respectful. This means listening, really listening, and putting yourself in your spouse's shoes. Work together to find resolutions to issues that address both of your major needs and desires.

3. Don't indulge in fairy tales about marriage because it's a no-win outlook. Be realistic.

4. Always schedule time for fun together.

5. Give each other the freedom to be with clients or friends even on a Friday night. Let your spouse do the things that enhance his life. You do the same for yourself. "I might even encourage him to go out with other people if he hasn't been out with friends in a while. He is the same way."

6. Anticipate your spouse's needs in difficult situations and take the reins if at all possible. The appreciation this engenders is well worth all the effort.

7. Talk openly about the serious issues and find resolutions together.

    A lesser relationship might not have survived the long-distance marriage that Leslie and Steve temporarily endured. Leslie dealt with her fears directly *with* Steve. Because of her direct communication style, Steve was able to understand how she felt, and together they crafted a solution.

    The best part is that now that they are back to normal, Leslie can see the gifts that the separation gave to them, which leads us to the last rule for your own garden.

8. Appreciate what you have and appreciate each other. Enjoy each and every day. In other words, take time to smell the roses.

Before selecting the site for your garden,
you need to decide how big it should be,
and you need to be certain
there is adequate sunlight.

Chapter • Four

Maureen

Maureen was born to an Irish Catholic family in Spring Lake, New Jersey, in 1960. Her mom was a tough cookie. Maureen saw her mother, like so many other mothers, as a nonstop doer. But Maureen's mom was different for her time—in addition to keeping an immaculate home, caring for the children, and cooking, she handled the checkbook and filed the income taxes. She was particularly unique for her time in that she obtained a master's degree when Maureen and her brother were young, and was a full-time teacher in the public school system where Maureen and her brother were educated. All the other moms on their street were stay-at-home moms. "Because we had more income, we did more…We went on vacation more. We had a smaller family and twice the income." The income her mother generated also enabled the family to acquire more possessions than other families in the neighborhood. "Other women felt a need for permission to buy something…not my mother."

Maureen's mom was neat and clean, with a firm belief in the old English saying 'A place for everything and everything in its place.' Maureen's mom was, and continues to be, a woman with a strong personality and drive. Her mom's sister was also a role model. Like her mother, Maureen's aunt worked and took care of her family. In Maureen's estimation, her aunt was definitely "a little softer around the edges" than Maureen's mom.

Maureen's Irish dad designed golf courses. Golf had not yet become a mainstream sport but was slowly gaining in popularity. Dinner was served to him upon his arrival home from work every night. "My father never did a load of laundry in his entire life," said Maureen, who loved him dearly. "Sometimes I can't rationally believe he is dead. My dad was a sweetheart."

It is no surprise that Maureen's concept of marriage was that the wife is a doer. "I thought that is just what you do." To a teenaged Maureen, the concept of the husband going to work and coming home every day seemed rather tedious. She wanted something more from her first marriage.

At the age of thirty, her act of rebellion took the form of a marriage to a boy-man unlike any of the men she knew. "My parents were very practical, and here was this guy who was a *little bad* and spoke a *little French*." Maureen chuckles, "You know, **all** the qualities you want in a partner! There was something that attracted me. He was different. The men I knew went to work and came home. There was something alluring about him. My role was to fix him because he needed to be fixed." (Did I mention that her boy husband chose not to work at all, ever?) "The marriage was going to work! Period! I was going to help him, fix him, and we were going to be fine. I was completely wrong on all counts." Their marriage lasted five years.

Her role in that marriage was as a caregiver, a constant nurturer, and in Maureen's succinct words, "a Mac [ATM] machine." Maureen learned the hard way that a husband can't be fixed by a nurturing spouse, especially if he doesn't think there is a need for improvement.

One pivotal day, Maureen was driving in a densely populated suburb, and she hit what I affectionately call *the* **saturation point**. She remembers the drive well. It was an emotional breakdown with full-throttle emotion and a realization that the nurturer in her had to be aborted. "I realized I couldn't do it anymore. I was done—DONE." There was no way she could continue. "It is very hard, when I think of myself as a good nurturing person, to make a decision to stop nurturing." This was Maureen's moment of clarification; when drastic change is needed and change is very close on the horizon, many of us will have such a moment.

Maureen will tell you that her second marriage to Scott was no act of rebellion like her first. She wanted a grown-up, a dependable man "who went to work every day," who contributed to the well-being of the marriage, and someone she could appreciate constantly.

In stark contrast of her previous marriage, Maureen can see that when spouses have a partnership and neither "needs" anything from each other, the world of possibilities for the relationship opens up. Growth for each person in a marriage like this is not only possible but also often encouraged by each other. This is marriage number two for both Scott and Maureen, and it is mutually supportive, blissful, loyal, and growing.

Maureen emphasized a seemingly unique but wise perspective, "I think one of the biggest myths about marriage is that it is a fifty-fifty partnership." On any given day, one person may give 100 percent and the other nothing...over time the averages may equal sixty-forty or fifty-five-forty-five or something even further from the myth of fifty-fifty. "If you are fundamentally disagreeing about something, and it is a yes or no question, when do you say, do it your way? When do you give up wanting to do it your way? When do you wait? For me, I have fundamental trust in Scott, and he is a smart guy. If he feels strongly that we should do something a particular way, I know he's looking out for us, so we do it his way."

The one fundamental truth or core of their marriage is that neither would ever do anything to hurt the other or to hurt their relationship. With this basic immutable trust, giving in to the other spouse's preference is really not a big deal. This is Maureen's way of saying that compromise really isn't a problem when you realize both parties are 100 percent supportive of each other and of the marriage. Neither Scott nor Maureen would ever make a decision that puts that in jeopardy.

Maureen will also tell you her marriage is not only about the partnership. "We have enormous respect [for each other], and we just like each other. Sometimes it is just that simple. We live with the fundamental truth that neither of us would ever do anything to intentionally hurt the other. If there are miscommunications or hard feelings, we remember that core."

Maureen remembers a day from her first marriage when she stood outside in a snowstorm scraping the snow off both her car and her husband's car. She didn't want to hear the excuse that he couldn't look for a job because it was snowing, and the car was snowed in. Today, Scott not only scrapes her car in a snowstorm, but also he will warm it up for her before she walks out the front door. That's a far cry from her first marriage.

Maureen says her husband does so much for her day in and day out, that she is happy to do all the cleaning and laundry. Maureen actually enjoys housework. (Go figure.) "To this day, I like cleaning my own house. I do it because Scott does so much. Can I keep a nice house? If I can just keep the house clean, do the ironing…it is a fair exchange of labor with Scott."

"We have so many different skills sets. That is what we like about each other. We complement each other. I don't know my times tables." (At this comment, I blurted out without much forethought, "You PUBLIC!" To which Maureen replied, "There is something exactly right about that! Fundamental math experiment in the Jersey schools in the 1970s!") Maureen graciously continued, "When he does crosswords, he'll know who the fourteenth president was, but he will ask me the composer of an 1859 opera…I'll have that." (As for me, I am still stuck on the thought that she may have married him for his knowledge of multiplication tables.)

They both admire and value each other's skill set. "He flew planes for a living. He is very responsible, very calm, very 'assess all information' and makes a decision pretty quickly." Scott organizes the kitchen and the house. "Our spices are in alphabetical order. We have a sweet and a savory spice rack—labels facing out. In the closet, clothes are arranged by color. I haven't lost my car keys in ten years."

When I ask Maureen about the role of religion for them, she replied, "Religion has played such a large role—it is the center thing in our home." Scott was raised in the Lutheran Church, but he was not involved with any organized religion when they first met. Scott converted to Catholicism after they married, but not because Maureen wanted him to be Catholic. "He would go to church with me and say 'I want to be in the spiritual place you are.'"

Because Maureen went to public school and received her Catholic education on Tuesday nights at Catholic Christian Doctrine Classes, she "never had the fear of religion like a lot of [her] friends." Maureen is referring to those friends who went to Catholic school and had "the fear of God" injected into them (THAT would be me!)

Scott had a different experience altogether. "He wanted to do the Rite of Christian Initiation of Adults by himself. He didn't want me to go with him. He wanted to be on that journey by himself." He learned a lot of the fundamentals of Catholicism that many who are born into it don't really learn.

When I asked Maureen what was the most fulfilling moment in her relationship with her husband, she responded, "I think there is one every day. I get fulfillment out of my relationship with his adult kids and grandkids. He sees that I love them." When Maureen first met Scott's children, they were adults and this was during a time when Scott was not yet seeing his children as adults. Some minor conflict arose over that, but it dissipated with time. Scott, like a typical father, needed some time to adjust to the maturity of his children.

Today Maureen has an adult relationship with her husband, in which they "shoulder the loads" of life together, like bills, the death of Maureen's father, and Scott's mother's illness. And they share the joys of family, especially Scott's biological children and grandchildren. "Nothing was completely my responsibility...that happened pretty early on. The bills were paid, and I wasn't the only one worried about them. We had expectations of each other regarding our families, and those expectations were met. I'd say things like, 'Let's call your mom and dad.' "

The day Scott's mom went into the Alzheimer's wing was difficult. Scott is one of five children. His father finally made the decision that she needed to be admitted. It was a long, difficult decision for him, and Maureen says it probably should have been reached earlier. When his father was finally ready, he needed Scott and his other children to support him. Maureen and Scott made the long drive from Philadelphia to Columbus, Ohio, to be there with Scott's parents. When they arrived, Scott called each sibling on behalf of his father. The day after his mother was admitted, he and Maureen were still at the hotel. Scott awoke in the middle of the night tormented by painful emotions. Maureen did whatever she could to console him and took some matters into her own hands. "I called his kids and said, 'I don't do this very often, but call your father.'"

Regarding this experience, Maureen empathizes, "It is almost worse than a death because you lose your mom and you see her lose herself. It is so horrible and so undignified. There are twelve women in there. She is the only one who was there three years ago. He [Scott's dad] goes to visit her every day. He is documenting their relationship." Scott's father is writing a blog about his wife and their experience. Maureen's heart aches both for Scott and for his father who is just watching his once vibrant wife languish day after day.

On the good side of life, Maureen will tell you, "One of my most cherished things is the relationship Scott had with my dad.

They would go to Atlantic City together. They would go play pool or cards—they were friends. That was a wonderful gift to me."

Both Maureen and Scott keep a journal that they write in daily. They call it the My Favorite Things journal, and in it they write about what their spouse did during the course of the day that was really appreciated. In this manner, they take time to regularly acknowledge how grateful they are for one another, and how much they value the other's contribution.

Maureen's gifts for your rose garden:

1. Have shared expectations.
2. Foster a strong ability to communicate. Talk. Work on good communication skills.
3. Make it a fundamental truth that neither party would ever do anything to hurt the other.
4. Do not foster the attitude I have to be right. Assume that there is not a right way but rather a your way, my way, and the way you decide on together.
5. Love each other's family as much as you love your own (IF at all possible).
6. Don't assume that your marriage needs to be a fifty-fifty partnership for it to work. Don't look for parity in all things. Maureen feels fifty-fifty marriages are a myth.
7. Take time to contemplate the good you see in your spouse, and from time to time, communicate those observations to your spouse. Consider establishing a My Favorite Things journal similar to Maureen and Scott's in which you will record what your husband did that day that you really appreciated. He will do the same for you. Reciprocity in a marriage is a key ingredient for a husband and a wife to be happy together.

Roses are known the world over
and there are over 100 species.
Do you know the differences and
do you know what kind you want in your
garden?

Chapter • Five

Dinah

Dinah was born in 1964 to a nontraditional family in East Lansing, Michigan. She has a brother who is three years older. Her parents divorced when she was six. Dinah has no memories of her two biological parents' relating in her early years and believes this lack of memory is a coping mechanism.

Her mother was a "raving alcoholic," and Dinah remained in her mother's custody, which was the norm at the time, until her father remarried when she was in the sixth grade. When her father had settled into his new, happy life, Dinah welcomed the opportunity to leave her mother and have a fully "intact family." At that time, she voluntarily moved in with her father, his new wife, and her two new stepsisters. Her older brother joined the family as well. They both wanted to be out of the mother's destructive home.

Dinah describes her biological mother as dysfunctional, but she will also tell you that her mother was an affectionate nurturer who loved to hug her daughter, and she was a good listener. That being said, during most of her childhood, Dinah was neglected. Fortunately, Dinah is quick to add, there was no physical abuse.

Dinah believes that every decision she makes as an adult in her own family is driven by her exposure to an alcoholic parent during her most formative years. She is determined to be a different kind of mother for her children. In fact, she has always had a very concrete picture of who she should be for her family and a full-time working mom isn't part of her vision. She knows rationally that millions of mothers work and "do it all," but that lifestyle is understandably not okay for Dinah's family. However, now that her girls are aged thirteen and fifteen, Dinah feels that the foundation for them has been set, and she is seriously considering reentering the workforce.

Dinah credits her stepmom with being loving and good to Dinah as well as her own children. Her stepmom took over the role of mother/caretaker and also helped Dinah learn to make good decisions. Unlike Dinah's biological mother, her stepmother was a working mom who didn't compromise her caretaking in any way. Her new parents were good at working out rules to make a healthy stable home for the children.

But her stepmom would get angry when her father worked too much. He was always a doer even when he was at home, whether it was mowing the lawn or fixing something in the house. He had to be active. He had to be doing something, and his wife wanted more personal time and attention than he was inclined to give.

When Dinah was a freshman in college and her father was fifty-seven, her parents divorced. Dinah hadn't seen the divorce coming.

As a young girl Dinah emulated the passions of her biological mother who had focused on the gender issues of that era that needed to be changed. Dinah became involved in women's lib, and was passionate about working on changing gender roles toward a more egalitarian reality. Dinah had a mission, "I took that on."

Her indignation surrounding this issue started early on. She remembers being really appalled as a young girl at the way a Tide® TV commercial depicted the woman of the house. The wife was the sole person in the house washing clothes for the husband and kids. She decided to take action. She prepared a survey and stood in front of the local furniture store to tell people about the commercial. Her goal was not only to get their opinions, but also to get their signatures protesting the commercial. "I was serious," says Dinah, who was about ten-years-old.

She also attended a young author's conference during this time period. Each child was required to write a book and exchange it with the others. Dinah's book was cleverly titled

Ms. Me. She was so excited about her title that she lay awake at night thinking about it. Today she barely remembers the book's content other than it was all about feminism and the role of women in our society.

As you can imagine, this same young girl had very strong opinions about marriage. "Early on I saw marriage as a little stifling—especially the expectation of the wife as caring for the husband since [it was the] early 70s. We were just coming out of the civil rights and women's movements." Dinah's thoughts were adamant, "I am sure as hell never hooking up with a man who is going to tell me what to do with my life!"

As for female role models who were good wives, Dinah cannot recall anyone she wanted to emulate. "Growing up there was not anyone other than Claire Huxtable from the Cosby Show!"

Over the years, she changed, softening some and certainly did so by college. Her thoughts about marriage were becoming very different than her childhood thoughts. In fact, Dinah feels that her thoughts about marriage became the exact opposite of what she had as a child. "I always knew I wanted a life-long partner, and I knew what it [marriage] should not look like," especially after seeing her father divorce again. "For me, it took on this idea that if I got married, it would be for life." Given all of her family life experiences, Dinah had a very clear idea of what her own marriage needed to be.

Dinah attended college in the state of Washington. She and James started dating her freshman year in college. She had a class with a mutual female friend. "James tells me he saw me working in the dining hall and wanted to meet me. She introduced us." They were engaged for a year and half, and married three years after graduating. Dinah was twenty-five. Their first of two daughters was born when Dinah was thirty.

"My expectation was that we would have lots of respect for one another. We would be completely honest and open with one another. We would always love to be with each other, always like each other, but not necessarily be best friends." By the time they married, Dinah was confident that they could be life-long intimate partners, but this confidence did not arrive without dialogue and careful assessment.

"We talked about having kids, religion, and race. My mother was white, dad was black, and my stepmom was white. I was adamant that James [a black man] had to accept my white family. There was a period early on when I was worried about whether or not he could deal with it." Dinah was enormously relieved and can happily report, "It has turned out not to be an issue."

Religion does play a role for them, but it does not yet have a settled role. "We definitely discussed it before marriage, but it was always about what we had as children. We didn't really [discuss] enough how we would deal with religion with our children, and it has been an issue. I grew up with no religion as a child, and he grew up with religion."

Dinah's paternal grandfather was an African Methodist Episcopal (AME) minister. In Dinah's words, "by the time, he [her father] had children, my father was done with organized religion. He had had enough. My mom never thought religion was important." James's background was very different. "As we have gotten older, I see James falling back into the messages he got as a child... Baptist to AME, they bounced around Christianity."

"As our children grow up and as I get older, I feel very spiritually connected...I've always believed that there is something more powerful than we on this earth." Her second pregnancy solidified this belief for her. "It was a difficult time because I was working full time and was overwhelmed." In fact, Dinah was living the exact life she most feared. She was far along in her pregnancy and driving home from work, not thinking of much really, when she was suddenly overwhelmed by the smell of Chantilly, her birth mother's perfume. Her mom had been dead for seven years, enough time that thoughts of her were not a daily occur-rence. Dinah rolled the windows down, but the car still smelled of Chantilly. She stopped for gas, and the smell was still there when she got back into the car. "Between the gas station and home, it dissipated. Her spirit was there…it was very odd." By that point in the ride, Dinah was crying. "Because I didn't grow up with her as support, it was so strange. She wasn't that kind of figure in my life, but it was a period in my life when I was highly stressed…" It didn't take long to realize how much pressure she was under. Despite her shock, she found "something about [her mother's] spirit was comforting."

Dinah realized from this experience that, "I have the ability to have faith." To Dinah, this was the kind of experience that solidi-fies one's belief in a greater power, and "As you get older, you realize there are very few coincidences."

Although Dinah feels a strong connection with things of the spirit today, during their courtship, "We didn't talk enough about religion. I have spearheaded our effort to try to be part of a church." But despite their repeated attempts, Dinah has not yet found a congregation that is perfect for her and her family. "I have guilt…my children don't know the Bible. There have been times when I felt at a loss when there is a reference to a Bible verse. I cannot participate in the discussion. I want something different. My children were not baptized. We've had many attempts to find a church. I have all these moral standards that may have come from my mother. For instance, one church we had been going to and liked a lot…has rules that do not allow women to be pastors. I can't do it. I bring my two daughters, and they are getting the message that they cannot be everything they could possibly want to be? They can't be a minister? There are certain things I cannot live with. I get pretty high and mighty."

They had very promising expectations of another church, too. "We went (to the church) right after Obama was elected. His election was a huge thing in our lives. It was so positive." At this service, the minister focused on the sin of abortion. He said, "If you had committed this sin, we need you to ask for forgiveness right now." Dinah was really disturbed by this. All she could think about during that service were the women in the church who had abortions and how the minister showed no compassion or understanding. She knew her husband agreed with her on this issue. His agreement, however, would not stop him from attending the church. "It doesn't bother him nearly to the degree it bothers me. He can get the good stuff and leave the other stuff. So we have bounced around a lot. Quite frankly I don't know if we will find any congregation. There are lots of ways to get to God. It doesn't have to be Christianity." I know that Dinah will keep searching.

When Dinah thinks about her childhood and what she gleaned from it for the plans for her life, she realizes how different her marriage and family could be. She says your background usually forms your cores values. If you come from a dysfunctional family, she says "either you take the dysfunction road or go to the polar opposite." In Dinah's case, she wisely and somewhat methodically took the opposite route. But she can still see the good that came from her early years. "I shouldn't sell my mother short. Her ideas were nonconformist, but she did give me the attitude that I can do whatever I want to do, and I don't have to put up with anything I don't want."

Dinah's role in her marriage is a vital one. She is the house manager, the primary care provider for the girls, the decision maker, and organizer. She is also "the strength and the glue that holds us together. I generally provide a calm level-headed approach. I don't always feel it, but that is what I portray."

With her twentieth wedding anniversary approaching, Dinah has been giving a lot of thought to what has made her marriage last. "This might sound trite, but I think before you even get to what contributes to a long-term marriage, you have to look at what kind of partner you are picking in the first place. I don't want to sound as if I know it all. I had some very clear-cut ideas about what I would not put up with, and I was determined. Any guy, in high school even, any guy who would say 'hey baby'…I had no time, no patience for and absolutely would not consider. I would never even date anyone who didn't have the potential characteristics I could respect and admire. During the time James and I dated, if I had ever gotten any indication that he was overly controlling or disrespectful…I'd have been so long gone." Some might say Dinah was lucky, but I say her luck stemmed from her disciplined discernment. "From the start I matched with someone who was a solid guy. Not only did he treat me with respect, but he had ambitions."

Dinah was interested to see how she and James handled social situations as a couple. "It was important to see James in social settings and see how he treated me in front of family, friends, and when he was around guys. I really also appreciated that he was comfortable in his own skin. And he didn't cower when he met my father."

Because of her childhood experiences, Dinah easily knew what she didn't want for herself, as well as what she needed in the relationship. James was the man who met her criteria. "We would not be here twenty years [later] if those things weren't in place before we got married."

Once the marriage decision was settled, they got down to the business of establishing a well-functioning family. To do this, Dinah feels strongly that honesty and good communication are critical ingredients, as is a strong partnership in all aspects of parenting. Although, because of James's work schedule and Dinah's being a hausfrau while the girls are young, she will tell you that "I have taken on more of that (daily parenting responsibilities) over the years."

They both also believe in "space apart" where they each can pursue individual interests. "We don't smother each other." Dinah knows that this has been a positive for their relationship. "You have to have that. You have the basis of something to discuss later in the day. Sometimes I don't think I have enough of that because I am not working, although I've done volunteer work in the past."

And true happiness according to Dinah requires two fundamental things—fun and more fun. "This is so important." For Dinah and James, all of these things have created a marriage where they "love to still be with just each other. I am shocked [by] couples who never even go on a date. They are always with kids or other couples. You need to be with each other, make each other laugh, be silly…We love to do weekends away."

In fact, they seem to do a lot of different things just with each other. They take a weekend to head to the nearby beach or to the Chesapeake. They dance whenever they have the opportunity. They love to take long walks together, dine out, and thrive on their long talks. Their shared experiences, combined with their intimacy, have created a language known only to them. A look, a word, a gesture, a phrase, or a wink communicates a universe of meaning that only they understand. "Our children have been one of the fundamental pieces of our marriage." When they share stories about the children, "[they] can look at one another and say just one word. You can't share…with anyone else in this way."

Before you think their marriage sounds like a perfect fairy tale, consider that James, a talented man with a prestigious job, unceremoniously received his walking papers. James was shocked beyond belief, as was Dinah, their families, and all of their friends. James was everyone's example of a successful professional. No one expected him to lose his job. All the fears that typically are associated with unemployment shook their sturdy foundation. What would they do about money? Would they be able to stay in their home? How would they afford their lifestyle? The job market was soft, and James's business was highly competitive. Would he find work? Would he find work locally? Would they have to move? How should they tell the children? The fear was overwhelming.

First, they told their young daughters. "The four of us sat in the family room, and we all cried." They told the girls, "We don't know what the outcome is going to be. We love you. We are staying together. There will always be a roof over your head and food on the table." Together as a family they saw each other's vulnerability, and they strengthened their bond as a result.

The next challenge was to get through the early days, one day at a time. These were the toughest days for James. Dinah held them both up those days. She would give him direction on what things to do each day such as "Honey, today you can clean the garage," and James would respond, "Okay. I can do that." Dinah took care of him while he processed what had occurred. Dinah will tell you that in the beginning, "I had total faith it would be okay." They did things like sit outside under the stars at night and talk or Dinah would share spiritual readings. During those first months of unemployment, Dinah was the glue that held them together.

When James started to "get his sea legs back," Dinah disintegrated. "He started to come around and that is when I fell apart and was a total mess." It was James's turn to carry Dinah. Their well-functioning partnership was now tested in adverse conditions.

James's unemployment was clearly the most challenging situation for their marriage. Today, with unemployment far behind them, Dinah says "this was a stressor, but I would take [it] any day over illness, although this was a big deal for us." Furthermore, she is unequivocal when she says that it was also the most fulfilling part of their lives together. She found a true gem in the midst of trouble. "I discovered this unbelievable ability for us to ying and yang each other." When James was down, Dinah propped him up, and when Dinah hit bottom, James reciprocated. They learned how to lean on each other in a time of crisis when a weaker marriage could have easily broken down.

But Dinah is quick to realize that they do not always do the ying - yang thing. They have had a couple of whopper fights. In these fights Dinah has experienced a blinding kind of anger. Still, she can find the silver lining here, too. "I've grown to realize that I can become so angry that I question staying together. I may not ever be able to fully forgive, but I have been able to heal. Realize that there are going to be times that you just flat out hate one another, but three months later you can be on the other side of it. It is cyclical and just what you do. You weather them. I don't have to panic now every time I am mad at him." There is an enormous maturity in accepting that married couples fight, that you may fight in your marriage, but that you work "to weather them" and get them behind you.

Dinah's wisdom acquired from her lifetime will give you a beautifully blooming garden:

1. Know what kind of spouse you want right out of the gate. At an absolute minimum, don't allow yourself to make the obvious mistakes. Remember Maureen from chapter 4 and the tough lessons she learned.

2. Make plans to avoid re-creating the bad raw stuff from your childhood. Replicate the good and alleviate the bad.

3. Talk about the important issues, like religion, early on if you want to avoid landmines in the future. Make at least tentative plans for how you would raise your children.

4. Always look for the good that comes out of every adversity. With Dinah and James, James's loss of his employment was utterly unexpected and devastating. They were completely uncertain as to what would happen next or where they would end up. Yet, as Dinah says, "I wouldn't change this experience for anything." That experience brought them so much closer as a couple and as a family. "I would not trade it for the world. It provided a new level of intimacy for us."

5. Do not immediately consider a fight, even a repeat and serious fight, as a reason to end your marriage. Consider the fight as something you might be able to weather. Just like the effect of the seasons on your garden, the cycles of your marriage will evolve.

6. Know your "strengtheners" and use them when you need them. Read the spiritual readings, or make the call to friends or family. Let yourself find support not only from your spouse but also from sources outside the immediate family.

7. Develop a partnership that fosters the ying – yang Dinah and James used when crises arrive.

8. Make sure the two of you have fun times. Schedule them into your calendar regularly.

9. When tough times hit, lean on each other, not away from each other.

Your garden needs you and all you
do to keep it blooming.
You find the sunny space.
You water.
You mulch.
You prune.
You feed.
You pamper.
You admire.
You love.

Chapter • Six

Gina was born in 1962 in a small river town of 5,800 households in Connecticut. Hers was a traditional childhood, complete with a working father and stay-at-home mom who raised Gina and her older brother.

"I always thought my mom was a good wife because [Dad] could be challenging. Mom always gave so much more than he did in terms of taking care of the kids, [caring for] him, the house. She carted us to all of our sports activities, which were nonstop—tennis in the fall, basketball in the winter, and softball in the spring. Mom was at every single game. We never saw Dad. I am not saying that that was a bad thing; I am saying that that was society. He was in the telephone industry and ended up having his own business with a partner. He traveled. Dinner was at seven, and if Dad wasn't home by seven, Mom fed us and would wait to have dinner with Dad…I didn't get to see much interaction between my parents as a kid because he traveled. They certainly talked about their days. There was communication, and I never saw fighting…. I think my parents knew who they were and grew together."

Gina's family is of loving, strong, Italian Catholic stock, promoting a very close-knit extended family with an emphasis on education and achievement. "My parents let us choose [whether we'd attend] the parochial school or the brand new high school." Both Gina and her brother chose the newer public school. Gina completed her formal education with a master's in business administration.

Gina can remember other families of her childhood, and it seems to Gina that some of the other parents fell short when compared to Gina's mother. "They really didn't support their family the way I think we were supported in terms of going to events, and financially...Mom would buy [whatever was needed] for me."

Gina always wanted to be married and wanted to have kids. "Unfortunately that didn't happen, but you can't have everything... I wanted to emulate Mom and the friendship that she had and has with her children. I wanted to replicate her very good home...I wanted to take care of everyone the way Mom did. And because of that, because of how I was raised, I was in a sorority and my nickname...they would call me Mom...When I was graduating, I got up in the morning, and the pledges had made a sign that said "We're gonna miss you, MOM!"

In stark contrast to her childhood dreams, Gina married for the first and only time at age forty-five and is breathtakingly happy. "It is interesting getting married [when you're] older because we knew who we were. If you don't know who you are, you have a real problem making that marriage work."

Gina and Kevin met in the bar at the Palm in New York. "I was out with my girlfriend for her birthday ...she wanted a Bolly-Stolly. I said '*Whatever*, it is your birthday. Let's go.' He was there. He was friends with the bartender. He had a drink and dinner at the bar. I ended up in the chair next to him. He wouldn't leave me alone. He was being friendly. I was difficult. He said 'I would like to take you to dinner.' I totally ignored it. As Maureen and I were leaving, he said, 'I still believe there is a question on the table.' I gave him my card and he called."

That encounter at a bar allowed some of Gina's childhood dreams to come to fruition and resulted in a union of unusual strength. Staying true to her vision of her mom as a wife, Gina's most significant characteristic as a wife is her nurturing nature. "He loves it, but it drives him crazy." For example, let's take dinner. "I am obsessed with planning our dinner, making sure I have something suitable every night, and that he is eating a balanced meal. I ask him what he wants. He says, 'I couldn't care less.' Sunday night is leftovers. I am definitely a planner. I definitely have to know what is happening for dinner."

Despite the fact that Gina's daily dinner obsession might make him batty, their marriage works because neither wants to change the other. Each party is happy to let the other be who he or she is to the fullest extent. This is part of the benefit of being more mature when you marry and *knowing who you are at the core*.

Before their marriage, Gina lost her job in an unexpected corporate reorganization. She had been a manager with significant responsibilities in the publishing industry since her early adulthood and was shocked and devastated to be unemployed. "I was independent and had my own financial security. My job defined who I was. I couldn't deal with it. He was my strength. When I called him, hysterically crying, running through the lobby…just how supportive he has been from that moment! He came right home from work and held me all day."

Gina's colleagues showed their respect, appreciation, and friendship by having a good-bye luncheon for her before her departure on December 31. Kevin proposed and gave Gina her ring the night before the luncheon. It was a wonderfully thoughtful way to launch Gina into a new and scary phase of life, letting her know how much she is loved and valued. Knowing that she was loved and that she and Kevin were committed to a future together helped Gina weather the upheaval of her career.

When I asked Gina about her expectations for her marriage, she said her primary expectation was that their feelings for one another and how they treat each other would not change. "Nothing changes just because you got married. You cannot change how you treat one another. You can't start to leave your clothes on the floor now…If you have the expectation you are going to change that person [your spouse] you are dead in the water."

Gina lost her job and became engaged to Kevin in December. Their next shocking trial came one month later, when Kevin's mother unexpectedly passed away. Spoken like a true optimist, Gina acknowledges the good in the adversity. "She was at peace because he had found somebody, and she knew I would take care of him."

But the loss of Gina's job and the death of Kevin's mother were not their only life stressors. Gina's father had been diagnosed with dementia. He was deteriorating rapidly, and Gina's mother was having trouble coping. Her family situation required and continues to require a great deal of Gina's time and support. She has expended much energy in caring for her parents and in working to find a suitable environment for her father's care. The very mother who so strongly nurtured her own children is now the beneficiary of all that she taught her amazing daughter. Gina is a selfless nurturer and is very happy to give to those to whom she is close.

Gina also happily gives credit to her husband for all that he does for her and her family. "That is something else that has been amazing in our relationship. We were having all these issues. I leaned on him and would not have made it through without him. We came together with our challenges to work thru them together instead of dealing with them on our own, pulling away from each other. That is really important. We can depend on each other."

Gina and Kevin not only drew strength from each other, but they rekindled their Catholic faith. As her parents had grown together many years ago over their own issues, Gina and Kevin are growing in their faith together. "Since our marriage, we go to church every Sunday, and it has become important to us, maybe because of everything we were jointly going through. Maybe all of these things just brought us full circle back to the church. It isn't one of us—it is both of us. We had that bond right out of the gate."

"We have our little Sunday thing now. We talk about what is relevant and how we can learn from it. After Mass we go to Starbucks, have coffee and a little breakfast sandwich, and talk about what is relevant. Father Peter is fantastic."

While they both have very separate professional lives, they also work well together. Kevin is launching a new business opening a twenty-first century health and fitness facility with state of the art equipment. There are a lot of decisions and stress associated with starting a new business. While Kevin has considerable expertise in the industry, Gina's business knowledge and taste for design are welcome additions to Kevin's business decisions. Gina offers her opinions, support, and dedication to his success in whatever way is needed.

Gina credits the happiness in their marriage to a couple of major attributes. Her first point is that they have enormous respect for one another. "We *respect* one another. We have *respect* for one another's feelings, what we are going through, how we treat each other, and how we want to be treated."

The second significant advantage is that they each have good communication skills and a strong desire to communicate. "We are able to talk when we are upset or mad or whatever. We are able to talk to each other. A voice may get raised a little from anxiety, but we do not escalate because, as adults, we are able to have a mature discussion as to 'why I am mad at you.' O yeah, we get mad at each other, but we don't storm out, and not speak to one another…We talk about it, address it, and move on." She stresses that even when you and your spouse cannot agree, you need to reach a resolution, and move past the problem. "AND don't bring it up again three months later. Three months later, you can't come out and say, 'You remember when you…'"

Gina has an additional bit of advice. "You have to have your priorities straight. My lifestyle over the last few years has changed dramatically. But I don't care if I am not going out for the $200 dinner; I am fine making chili and cornbread at home. What is important is that we are together. I didn't know I had THAT in me because I had 'my lifestyle.' Now, [our relationship] is what's important!"

Although Gina didn't stress the role of loyalty and trust, a lot can be gleaned from her talk of their love for one another. "Our love is unconditional. I know that I don't have to question his devotion."

Gina and Kevin had so many challenges in such a short time early in their relationship. Despite all these problems, and perhaps because of them, Gina and Kevin are a happy couple who are growing together every day. Their problems have made them stronger individually and as a couple. This attitude continues to be their reality despite all of life's challenges. "We are just as happy or happier today than we were before."

"Kevin and I always say that we are not like other couples. We are unique. We are different."

This is how Gina nurtures her rose garden:

1. Always communicate and force a resolution.
2. Know what your priorities are and make sure the first priority is your relationship.
3. When challenges arrive, as they undoubtedly will, lean on each other and support each other. Don't turn away from your spouse.
4. Understand each other's goals and talk about them. Support each other dreams and celebrate the successes.
5. Find and nurture joint interests, such as religion, curling (FINALLLY there is something we can blame on the Scottish besides the kilt), cooking, belly dancing, log racing, or yode-ling. (Did you know yodeling keeps the Martians away? Well not exactly, but it does blow them to smithereens, which I think is a noble family pursuit. After all, they have been scaring us for generations.)
6. When times get tough, take the day you are living and make it worthwhile *with your spouse*. Forget about what your problems might do to your tomorrows and realize you have something worth celebrating every day.

*A rose known as Little Mischief
is a hearty rose that blooms all season
and resists all diseases.*

Chapter • Seven

Leah

Leah was raised in a traditional family in a small Arizona town during the '60s. She has one sister who is four years her senior, and her mom stayed home until she felt the girls were old enough that she could help a little in the small family business. During Leah's childhood, she and her peers defined the wife's role as a nurturer of both her husband and children.

As a child, Leah remembers wanting children, but she was not interested in being a traditional wife. She viewed her mother and her friends' mothers primarily as housewives, and she had a burning desire for something more for herself. "I wanted to do something more for myself [that was] not in support of somebody else."

For adult role models, Leah looked to her teachers, many of whom were single and spinsters, and to a few women shop owners in her small town. She didn't have any exposure to women in bigger businesses or corporations. "I knew I wanted to be a business owner. I wasn't really sure when it was going to happen or in what form, but I did want it."

In regard to marriage, she knew from an early age that if she were to have the career she wanted, she would have to have a spouse who was supportive and with whom she could have a strong partnership. (Isn't it amazing to be so worldly wise as a young girl?) "It [having a partnership] was on my mind the whole time because [becoming] a young adult in the late '70s and early '80s, I knew that a career wasn't the straight-line approach…I would need to have somebody in partnership to have a career." In early adulthood, Leah was not only self-aware but also understood the society in which she lived and how her desires didn't quite mesh with mainstream expectations. She realized that not every woman of her era wanted the career she so intensely desired, and she knew that a different kind of partnership would be needed for her marriage and career to work in tandem.

In her early twenties, Leah married with the sound expectation that the union would create a team of two and that each person would be supportive of the other's career and personal life. Her young husband was as driven in his career pursuit, perhaps even more so than Leah. During their joint years in graduate school, he was focused on getting into medical school. When he was accepted, he became completely consumed with his studies. He didn't want to be involved in anything else. They grew apart, and the marriage ended.

Leah's second marriage lasted seventeen years. As long as times were good, they encouraged and supported each other. When times were not good, the marriage suffered.

They had totally incompatible ideas about the most basic family ideal: having children. Leah's life-long dreams of being a mother clashed with her husband's reluctance to give up their DINK (dual income no kids) lifestyle. (If you are a traditional human who is easily offended, I suggest you NOT look up *dink* in the *Urban Dictionary*. It is a jaw dropper, albeit somewhat entertaining).

Leah pushed hard to have a child, and when their only child was born, her husband went into a deep depression that lingered for over a year. These emotional periods of gloom would also set in later on when financial and business problems developed. His bouts of depression would hit him very deeply and suddenly.

Depression wasn't their only problem. During a very difficult time in Leah's business, a significant wedge grew between them. "When our business was going under and our former best friend walked off with hundreds of thousands of dollars of our money… that was a turning point. My formerly supportive husband completely removed himself from me, our marriage, our business, and our future. It was a terrible time, and I felt I had to solve all of the problems myself. I broke down every day."

But the biggest difficulty for their marriage, a difficulty that proved insurmountable, was her husband's affair. He had a lengthy sexual relationship with one of his coworkers. Leah knew the woman, had been in her home socially, and had met her four children. "At one point I knew he was infatuated with her, but I didn't think he had the guts to do anything about it." By the time their secret became known, he and his girlfriend were strategically planning the end of their marriages and the beginning of their lives together.

When Leah looks back on her second marriage, she says that her husband was a good husband, and that the first six or so years of the marriage were good ones; she believed he was a nearly perfect mate for her. During her pregnancy, the marriage became a little rocky. By the time their son was nine, and her husband's affair was revealed, they agreed to separate. There was no custody battle. Her husband was moving fifty miles away to be closer to his girlfriend. Although Leah did have to pay her husband in the divorce settlement, the proceedings were not contentious.

Leah, however, knew that she had some changes to make. The marriage took its toll on her self-esteem, and she was left feeling unappreciated and unattractive. She had considerable self-doubt, and it took her a while to realize that these feelings of inadequacy weren't based on fact. If you knew Leah, you, too, would realize just how absurd these thoughts are. (The Little Mischief Rose is beautiful in sight and in scent).

Leah will tell you that she doesn't know how she managed to "snap out of it," but she clearly does know. "Realizing it had very little to do with me…**that** took a long time. I tapped [into] my strengths as an independent person and independent business owner."

During this period of separation, Leah also spent a considerable amount of time planning "how my son and I were going to continue—physically, school wise, financially, in a new neighborhood—and subsequently made very good decisions that allowed me to focus on him and not materials things."

With time and her inner strength, she came to realize that the breakdown of the marriage was not about her. The affair was about him, what he needed, and what he would do to get what he needed. That second, seventeen-year marriage is years in the past now, but she and her ex-husband have an amiable relationship focused on raising their son.

Leah did meet another man who is very different than the men of her past. They lived together for two years, and when he proposed, Leah was shocked speechless. In the immediate instant following his proposal, she remembers clearly a voice flashing through her head that said, "NO. I don't ever want to get married again!" But that voice was fleeting. She realized that what she wanted most was for the man she loved to be happy. Their relationship was strong and could be even stronger in a marriage. Formalizing their relationship with wedding vows would be beneficial for both her teenage son and his teenage children. Finally, and most definitely as the last consideration, she realized it would be good for her. This year they will celebrate their second wedding anniversary.

Especially after the demise of her second marriage, she knew it would take a very confident man to make a good match with her. Her ideal mate would be a strong, independent man with his own life, self-confidence, and a strong sense of self. As Leah put it, in her second marriage, she was the alpha and her husband was the beta. In her current marriage, she is the alpha at work, where she continues to run her own successful business, and the beta at home. "This works for me, and I do not feel conflicted in any way."

Importantly, they share core values as is illustrated by their approach to raising their respective children. "A happy marriage requires both parties wanting to be a partnership, part of a team whether it is for hobbies, financial reasons, raising a family, or simply life enjoyment. My current husband and I both feel that raising our children is a high priority, and we strive to give our teenage sons attention and help them become independent human beings."

From the beginning of this marriage, her husband showed how much he valued their relationship by being clear that he wanted to work on and always strengthen their partnership. They fortify their marriage through activities that include traveling, nights out without the children, and jointly raising and training a dog.

As a consummate professional, Leah rarely talks with her clients about her personal life. But when the topic does arise, and she tells them she is on her third marriage, they are "flabbergasted and speechless." Leah will say to them, "I know. I know. You don't even have to say it. You see me as stable, a good head on my shoulders, and kind of sweet. I am the last person you would expect to be married for the third time." She says, "Just because I have been married three times doesn't mean I am wild or screwed up. It doesn't mean those things at all." Leah wants everyone to know, especially those who have never divorced, that you probably harbor one major presumption that is very far from the truth. Some people believe and are quick to state that divorce is a shared responsibility. Leah says, "If it were fifty-fifty, the marriage would have worked. The problem is that it wasn't."

Leah's garden is full of strong rosebushes because of some hard-earned knowledge:

1. Create your own life where you have a lot of control. Then and only then can you compromise and be a good listener and support person at home. You need self-confidence and independence to be a good partner!

2. Make sure you and your betrothed share core values. (Forgive me this one, but as the nuns always said, "repetition is the mother of all learning.")

3. Enhance your existing relationship by honoring your shared values, fostering strong communication, and creating fun times and loving intimacy.

4. When one partner wants out or "sees the exit sign flashing" get it through your head that it is already OVER!

5. When it is over, focus on the important things you need to do such as deciding where you will live and what changes are needed for the children, and on the areas where you are in control such as your career. Take positive action toward your new life.

6. Allow yourself to explore another relationship when one fails. Don't allow yourself to become bitter or a victim. Take what you have learned and make the next relationship a better one.

*Roses relish fertilizer, especially fertilizer
with well-rotten manure.
Manure fosters robust growth
and fabulous flowers.*

Chapter • Eight

Jessie was born in 1973 in a small town on the outskirts of San Francisco to a middle class family; she had four older siblings. Her parents were together for a long time but divorced when she was six. Jessie sees the divorce as a good decision for her mother.

Her dad was a traditional Italian guy who worked in his parents' flower shop and greenhouses. Jessie's mother also worked in the family business. Both sets of grandparents and Jessie's family lived on the same street. None of her grandparents were warm people. They all were traditional and "old school."

Her father's parents played an especially important role in Jessie's life until the divorce. They were a steadfast component in their daily lives because everyone was involved in the family business. But her mom grew very tired of having her in-laws so integrally involved in her immediate family life.

"My mom divorced and ended up living with a woman in a platonic relationship, but if the time had been different they would have had a physical relationship. Our social status plummeted as a result of the divorce. Dad hid money in the business, and we had a tough time with no money. [My mother] had to go to a factory." Eventually, Jessie's mother enrolled in a refresher course in nursing and resumed that career.

"Mom got the raw end of the deal, and she cultivated that herself. In my view, Dad was a jerk, not progressive, and had a lot of issues, but he was not the demon she made him out to be. She didn't take ownership of her own issues. She got into a marriage she didn't like, didn't work to change herself, and projected her misery on him. It couldn't be 'we really have different views of the world, let's get a divorce.' No. He had to be evil for her to get out of the marriage."

Her mother's girlfriend, Mary, was enormously instrumental in Jessie's life. Her presence and her outlook gave Jessie an expanded view of the world. She also helped provide some financial stability, although money was tight, and she helped create a sense of family. "We would spend summers with Mary's mother; Mary's mom was a real grandmother."

Jessie's mother lived with Mary until Mary died of cancer when Jessie was a teenager. Had Mary's cancer not been terminal, "she would have been with us forever."

As a result of the divorce, her father's parents disowned her mother, as well as all five of their grandchildren. "My mom's parents did for a short time as well…divorce was a sin; you make your bed you lie in it." But her maternal grandparents reunited with their daughter and their grandchildren when Jessie was ten.

Given her grandparents, her mother, Mary, and Mary's mother, Jessie did not get a positive perspective of marriage as a youngster. "Just looking at my mom and other women—no one seemed happy…all complained about their husbands. There were not a lot of good role models for marriage when I was a kid."

Her mother's relationship with Mary, however, opened Jessie's eyes "to more progressive relationships." It stimulated an intellect not shy of intense study and exploration. Jessie pursued a triple major in college. "One of my majors was women and gender studies. I had sexual relationships with women. I could do what I wanted to do."

Not only did her observations free her to dabble in alternative lifestyle liaisons, but Jessie also believes her nontraditional childhood significantly shaped her personal views on a wife's role. "What happened with my family made a nontraditional lifestyle okay. It was excoriated in our town [when I was] a child, but it had the opposite effect on me. It put me on a certain path that was intertwined with my intellectual path. I never want to get a divorce. If I married, I wanted it to be good…I wanted to marry a nontraditional man. I dated nontraditional men…I wanted a 'girlie man'—the opposite of my father."

There was another immutable component on Jessie's required list for her future marriage. She adamantly wanted a marriage where each spouse provided equally to the household.

"My mom took care of all the kids, [worked the] second shift, and *everything*." To Jessie this hard work came at a very significant cost. It seemed that her mother had no sense of herself, of who she really was, and she had no insight into her own behavior.

Jessie was determined not to recreate her mother's life and problems, and to that end, she has always valued self-understanding and development. Today, Jessie provides well for her family, and she does so with intelligence, self-awareness, self-analysis, and constant growth.

Despite all the lackluster relationships that surrounded Jessie as a child, Jessie always wanted to get married and always wanted to have children. And she always had boyfriends; sometimes there were multiple boyfriends simultaneously. She ended her relationship with her boyfriend from her high school and college years when he began to pressure her to have a baby. Although she knew she wanted children, it was clear to her that it was not the right time and he was not the right mate. She had other significant relationships that could have easily ended in marriage. Jessie says of this time in her life, "I had issues around 'pulling the trigger.'"

When she first met her husband, it was a hectic and crazy time in her life. She had a new job at a start-up company. And she was busy outside the office as well. She was involved in four different relationships with men who were largely Berkley graduates.

Thinking that they would really like one another, a mutual friend encouraged Jessie and Rob to meet. "Neither of us wanted a relationship at that time, but we really fell for each other. He never wanted to have kids, never wanted to be married, and wanted to live in the Caribbean. Now he lives near Colusa,

California, on an organic farm, is married, and has three kids. He changed his desires. It is interesting that I ended up with someone who didn't want the fundamentals I wanted. Finding out that he really didn't want kids...I thought he was joking...I was *so* in a different place. I remember the day I was driving home from a wedding shower... and [I was] crying, 'If there is a God, please give me a sign as to *what* I am suppose to do. I really love this guy.' But I wanted kids." Guidance arrived shortly thereafter in a most unexpected way. She made a surprising discovery in mid-August. Just days after that impassioned prayer, she realized that she was pregnant. Furthermore and unbeknownst to Jessie, Rob was secretly planning to propose over Labor Day.

"There wasn't a lot of thinking. I totally went on gut and intuition. We were gonna keep the baby. I figured it would all work out." But the universe had other plans. Jessie miscarried before their wedding day.

Jessie had expectations that their marriage would be a marriage of equality. Both spouses would work, and both spouses would take care of the children, but she also was very far from naïve. Remember that one of her majors was women and gender issues. She studied feminism. Her thesis was on women's participation in the Christian coalition. Jessie wanted to know "why would women participate in a movement that would ultimately undermine their interests? I thought a lot about women and the tradeoffs they make."

In regard to their marriage expectations, "We would have 'equal' whatever that meant. We were both working at the same company, and I thought we would live in the city somewhere. Life is **totally** different from what I expected."

By the time they married, her husband had a big Victorian house in San Francisco. He was working for a prestigious architectural firm, and Jessie was a vice president of human resources at a start-up company. Today they have a twenty-five acre farm far northeast of San Francisco. Her husband is a very happy organic farmer. His farming quite literally puts food on the table but generates no cash income for the family. Jessie has cleverly managed to structure her own consulting business to work only fifteen hours per week. She consults on strategy for human resource issues and is an executive and life coach. They live a gratifying life raising their children in a very rural setting. This transition did not, however, happen overnight, and it certainly did not happen without much consternation and, you guessed it, self-assessment.

Jessie and her husband married in September 2000. In July 2003, they had their first of three children. It was an unplanned pregnancy, and it was a very stressful time. Rob was not ready for fatherhood. Fortunately, today, Jessie doesn't hesitate for a second when she says, "He is a great father. He adores his kids."

Jessie had certain clear-cut expectations such as living in or near a city, having traditional jobs, raising the children jointly. But twists and turns in their marriage took them on a different path. Rob wanted a different way of life and to him that meant running an organic farm in the country. "For a long time...I felt conflicted...*That* is great! You want to be an organic farmer? So what does *that* mean?"

Jessie was working an intense job in the city while he was working the farm and taking care of the kids. Sometimes, in order to avoid the four-hour daily commute, she would stay at her mother's through the week. The stresses of this arrangement generated fissures in their marriage foundation that would have ended a lesser marriage. Jessie boils it down to, "Our marriage almost tanked."

First of all, there were problems with Jessie's mother being so closely involved in their daily lives. Jessie's mother would see how much Jessie was doing. Jessie was a hard-working executive; she was commuting excruciating long hours; she was a nursing mother of two demanding children. And the problem with her mother was like too many other mothers: she couldn't keep her mouth shut. Her mother was very vocal in stating that Jessie was doing too much, and her husband was doing too little.

Jessie knew that she wasn't happy, but her mother really wasn't doing anything positive to help. In contrast, her mom was working hard to drive wedges between Jessie and her husband, something Jessie has come to resent. "What she wasn't hearing was that I was not happy. I didn't want to be away from the kids, my husband, or be an executive. This was not the life we wanted, but mom had her own issues and she wouldn't hear what I wanted."

There was another very weighty stressor on their marriage. Staying true to their nontraditional attitudes, they had always talked about an open marriage, but Jessie felt somewhat blind-sided when she learned of Rob's affair. She asked about it, and he was forthright. That being said, "He didn't view it as an affair. He was surprised that I was surprised...[It was] horrible, but the best thing that ever happened." Jessie views the affair as "a wake-up call" regarding not only their marriage, but also the way of life they were sustaining. It made her stop and say, 'Wait. Do I want to be doing this?'

Ultimately, Jessie says she had, "no problem getting over the affair. We didn't have a traditional agreement. I had to ask. He didn't tell me. He didn't respect the woman he had an affair with...It was complicated. It was easy to get passed because once I found out about it, we talked about it, we moved to an agreement...It was hard, but it wasn't what it was for many women. It was a great inflection point in our relationship for me to look at what I wanted. I was working with a coach. It became a lens to look through my life."

As a result, Jessie took a three-month sabbatical. In order for her to do this, Rob took a job. Jessie saw this as a gift directly from him to her. "He was doing something he really hated for me, so that I wouldn't have anxiety over the money. I could figure out what I wanted. I ended up quitting my job," and she launched her own, now successful, consulting business.

All of the stresses on their marriage during the period when Jessie was traditionally employed pale in comparison with the pain that came next. And yet, Jessie is adamant that there is beauty despite the pain.

Their son, Elijah, was stillborn, and Jessie will tell you that it was one of the most fulfilling times of their marriage. "He [her husband] was really there for me. He was amazing. It was one of the times in my life I really felt loved, and I realized how much he loved me. Jessie had planned to give birth at home, but complications during labor forced a change of plans. "I had to go into the hospital. Labor was horrible. He was so 'present'...I didn't want the baby away from me. I did not [want him taken] to the morgue! Rob figured out how to get the baby home and bury him on the farm. It was a beautiful ceremony. It was exactly what I wanted, and Rob made all of that happen. He didn't ask me. He just knew and made it happen."

Rob was an enormous part of Jessie's strength despite her own very significant spirituality. "I didn't feel like I could really deal. I was physically exhausted and sick during labor with a fever." Jessie is unambiguous that Elijah's death was a horrible and devastating experience, but one with clearly identifiable gifts. "We are so much closer, and we appreciate our children so much more. This little baby brought us all this." This crisis was pivotal in their relationship, and they became stronger together as a result.

Both spirituality and self-development are now intrinsic components of their days. When they first met, Jessie considered herself an atheist, and traditional religion played no role in their lives except for a brief period of involvement in the Unitarian Church. She will also tell you that her husband had a sense of God before she did. Today Jessie says, "We both have a spirituality philosophy. I have learned so much from him, and he has really changed me. All conflicts that come up I view as an opportunity to change and grow."

The organic farming has taken her husband on his own spiritual journey that includes learning about sacred plant medicine, theories about plant intelligence, and shamanism. Jessie sees the parallels in their personal growth. "The more we grow, the closer our paths get…He is much more committed than I am to sustainability." He not only thinks and learns about organic farming, but he is very proactive and puts what he learns into what he grows. "He grows all our own food…I respect anything he wants to do. He figures it out and does it. I am much more of a perfectionist, so I won't do it. He is a good counterpoint to that. He is much more dogmatic. He lives his values. I am a little more anchored into the traditional world—401(k) stuff."

I asked Jessie what she would identify as her most defining characteristics as a wife. It was clear to me that she is very understanding. I think this comes from being so insightful. She realizes that we all are human and learning new lessons every day. She also is a huge advocate of taking responsibility for the role she plays within the marriage—the good and the bad. "All of my husband's friends say 'you are the luckiest guy in the world.' I am pretty flexible and understanding, and I take ownership, but I am not flexible about stuff regarding my kids. I have pretty dogmatic ideas about that."

She believes in being sure that her children's minds, hearts, and hands are educated, a philosophy that is exemplified by the private school they attend. She wants her children (they now have three) to thrive spiritually, intellectually, and emotionally. It is her strong belief that education is "not just about brains."

True happiness in a marriage usually requires similar values, Jessie believes, but you don't have to agree on everything. In Jessie and Rob's case, both pursue life as a learning experience and this attitude underlies everything in life for them and has proven to be important in their sustaining their marriage.

Having "a similar world view" greatly enhances your prospects for happiness and longevity in a marriage. Thankfully, Jessie and her husband both believe in finding the gifts in any and every adversity. This joint outlook is another component that helps to make their marriage strong. If Jessie or her spouse believed the stillbirth was nothing more than a devastating, immobilizing, and senseless tragedy, their marriage, or any marriage for that matter, might not have survived the strain.

They have also learned how to give and take. "Overtime we have done more of that." When Jessie had their last child, she took some time off of work. Rob offered to pursue a traditional job again during this period. "But I said no because he is so miserable (when working a traditional job). I happen to like my work, and it happens to make a lot of money."

Jessie can list the most important growth and strengthening times in their relationship. Chronologically, the first was the affair. This was a time they both revisited their relationship, and emotionally and intellectually recommitted to one another.

In keeping with Jessie's ongoing quest for personal enhancement, she attended a specialized, weeklong residential course for intensive personal discovery and development. This was a special place where Jessie, of her own admission, came to "own more of my stuff." She has also spent considerable time exploring spirituality. Jessie credits all this with an enormous positive effect on her personally and on her marriage.

The third and no doubt the more heart-wrenching time was the death of Elijah, and the gifts they have embraced from this tragedy.

Jessie's gifts from their organic garden:

1. Develop strong communication skills. (Have we heard this one before?)
2. Foster a sense of humor. (Sounds familiar).
3. Have a sense of your own fallibility. "You can't always be thinking about trying to make yourself right. Also look at it from your husband's perspective."
4. You need to have flexibility. The world, and consequently your own life, is changing regularly, whether you see it or not. Not everything will be under your control. Learn how to adapt. Roses can show you how. Some learn to climb, some grow freely, some take the shape of a bush, some take the shape of a tree, and some crawl along as ground cover.
5. Learn how to give and to take within your marriage.
6. "You shouldn't look to your husband to be the end all and be all of your life. It is okay and even healthy to have different interests, other friends, etc." Have a life beyond the life of your marriage. It adds a dimension not only to you personally but also to your relationship.
7. Always let the situation happen. Feel the feelings. Ask yourself, "What is the gift that I can take away?" In the words of Jessie, "Otherwise, you get stuck in your story about this horrible thing that happened. Don't be the victim."

*Did you know that
another name for rose garden
or bed of roses
is a
rosary?*

Chapter • Nine

Estelle

Estelle was born two years before the great stock market crash of 1929. (Trust me. She had nothing to do with it). Although she has had a few health issues, she is still a pretty woman with a sharp mind and a sense of humor. She is the beloved mother of three doting children, and she is close to each of them. She lives with her youngest daughter, a single mother of two young men.

Estelle, the middle child of three, grew up in the Frankford section of Philadelphia, walking to school each day. She graduated high school, which was a notable accomplishment in 1945, at the age of eighteen.

Estelle's mother, the oldest of six children and one of only two girls, was raised as a "princess" and was Estelle's major role model. She also remembers an outgoing and vivacious maternal grandmother.

As we've seen, at this time, women were expected to get married, and young wives could anticipate that their husbands would provide financially for the family. But as Estelle points out, men did not get off scot-free. In fact, they had constraints of their own, mores that influenced their daily behavior. The men of Estelle's youth were not expected to show any detectable expression of emotion. Rather, society encouraged men to suppress, or flat out deny, any emotions, thus displaying a true sign of manliness, control, and strength.

Estelle cannot recall any overt affection or romance between her parents. In fact, her childhood memories reveal a stormy marriage; her father was significantly older than her mother, he worked hard, and had strong expectations as to what should happen in the home.

Because dad worked in the order department for a baking business, there was always food on the table despite the rocky financial environment. He was a devoted and good father who always had a car and would drive them to Atlantic City. Estelle fondly remembers using the lockers under the boardwalk for twenty-five cents a day.

Estelle's paternal grandmother spoke only Polish, which made communication difficult with her grandchildren. Estelle's entire family would visit her every Sunday. The adult menu was coffee and rye bread.

Estelle's father died quite unexpectedly at age thirty-nine. Estelle was twelve, her sister was fifteen, and her brother was only six. Her dad's premature death made life very different and very difficult. Suddenly, Estelle's "princess" mother was alone with children to feed and care for. There was life insurance, but it provided only enough to pay funeral expenses. There was no such thing as Social Security, so her mother was forced to go to work. Estelle's mother was strong and handled the difficulty with grace. Through the kindness of a good neighbor, her mother found work on an assembly line and later as a foreman's clerk. Another kindly gentleman drove her to work each day. The family had no car and even if they had, Estelle's mother didn't know how to drive. Public transportation was the means of getting around when the distance was too far to walk.

Estelle's mom was not only strong but also proud. Charity provided their butter, bread, and bags of flour. The flour enabled her to bake for the family when she got home from a day's work. The children were told that they were to tell no one they regularly received this charity.

When Estelle was nineteen she met her husband who was seven years her senior. A year later they were married, but during that year they didn't see much of each other because her betrothed, who was serving in the Marine Corps, was on a ship.

Estelle recalls having absolutely no expectations of the marriage. She was completely and utterly in love, had total trust in her young husband, and was ready for whatever their life would bring for them together. She knew she wanted to be the perfect wife for him, someone he loved to introduce to his friends.

They married in November of 1946, and Estelle gave birth to their daughter Patricia in 1948. Four years later, Estelle gave birth to Cyndee and their son, Stephen, followed in six years. Her husband was home to witness only Stephen's birth. Most of his time was spent completing tours of duty in Korea, Vietnam, and Japan.

One year after Stephen's birth, the love of Estelle's life was diagnosed with leukemia while he was on duty in Virginia. He was facing it alone in a place that seemed very far away, and they were both in shock. Estelle kept asking, "How can this be happening? Will I have the strength? He had been in Las Vegas when they did the atom bomb testing. They were supposed to have been okay, but he was diagnosed with leukemia, and many people believe it was because of the testing." There was very little scientific understanding of the disease at that time, and all treatments were experimental.

Initially, the doctor thought he would have only six months to live. He, however, defied the doctor's knowledge and lived three additional years. To Estelle, it seemed that his health during these three years had half year cycles: six months of doing well and six months of decline. Yet, Estelle will tell you that throughout this period, "We didn't believe it." Estelle prayed and went to Mass every day.

Toward the end, he spent the majority of his time in the naval hospital. During his last three weeks, Estelle stayed with him at the hospital. The girls were in school and a neighbor took care of them. Stephen, now four years old, stayed with Estelle's sister.

Despite the support provided by her family and the fortitude from her faith, Estelle couldn't shake the feeling that people were judging her and that she was being punished for something. This was an enormously difficult time for Estelle, and the parallels between her father's early death and her mother's struggles, and her own husband's death and her hardships were chilling. The strength her mother, also a mother of three, illustrated during her ordeal was the same strength that Estelle needed to tap within herself to survive her own heartbreaking trial.

As her mother did before her, she set off to find employment. For a while she worked in real estate and as a secretary in the U.S. Army Corp of Engineers where she stayed until retirement at age sixty-two.

Estelle was very active in her church community after the death of her first husband. At the church bowling league, she met Frank, an earnest man and childless widower, who was sixteen years her senior. His wife had passed away three years earlier. They began to date.

He was a bit "old world" and believed it was the man's place to handle everything. He really would have to grow to come into an existing family, but Estelle was willing and hoping. "I prayed that Frank would accept the children." They married and their gratifying marriage lasted until Frank passed away some twenty-one years later.

When he married Estelle, Frank fully embraced fatherhood and each of Estelle's children. He handled his corresponding parental responsibilities with vigor. Estelle's oldest, Patricia, was already out of the house and living a fast life in New York City, but Frank was a disciplinarian not unlike her biological father. While Patricia was doing what she wanted to do when in New York, there were different expectations of her when she came home to Pennsylvania to visit. If she was out after midnight, she would be locked out of the house. Patricia was the one who "pushed the envelope" with both Frank and her mother. Today, even Patricia, a sixty-something beauty who maintains her model-like perfection, will tell you, "I was a brat."

Despite his love for the children, Frank never formally adopted them because they would have lost the military benefits they received as result of their father's death. But he did support them financially. This enabled Stephen, who benefited by being younger, to save all his benefits. By the time he reached adulthood, he had a nice nest egg as the direct result of Frank's generosity. Stephen benefited in more ways than financial. He was only four-years-old when his biological father passed away, and in Estelle's words, "Frank was really his father."

Cyndee, the younger daughter, took the death of her father very hard, and her recovery was a very long time in coming. She was not very accepting of the new man in her mother's life. Despite being the "perfect Catholic school girl" who was involved in everything, she had a strong desire to escape the real world as soon as she was able to make her own decisions. After high school, she entered a convent in a quest for religion to cure her aching soul. After two years, she returned to her family, including Frank. Not long afterward she was emotionally ready to embark on her own marriage and children.

Estelle knows that she was a different wife the second time around. She was older and had gained a great deal of experience from taking care of the children, maintaining a stable home, and earning a living. During her first marriage, she was responsible for most of the day-to-day living issues, but her young husband was still very influential and had firm expectations regarding his home and family while he was away.

But Frank was a different man altogether. While Frank and Estelle's first husband shared a love for discipline, Frank was of a different generation and believed strongly in being the man of the house. He was certainly more available to contribute and to take on leadership roles and family duties, for which Estelle was grateful.

The second marriage was also easier because there were fewer responsibilities in general. The children were older, and finances were better. They had time and money to go on vacations, and they regularly enjoyed cruises.

Estelle found that neither she nor Frank expected more than the other could give. The expectations they had of each other were realistic. This frame of mind isn't likely to come without maturity and some degree of experience. Moreover, they both wanted and valued the relationship and the companionship.

Sweet, loving, and generous Frank passed away because of an abdominal aneurism after twenty-one years of marriage to Estelle.

Religion continues to play a big role in Estelle's life. Estelle, like many Catholic women of her generation, my mother having been one as well, dutifully says the Rosary every day.

Estelle's sage gifts for your rose garden:

1. You have to have good sex. "This [sex] should not be a reason for the end of a marriage. A man should not have to stray."
2. A common religion is a big strength to any marriage. If you are fortunate enough to have a common religion, you should nurture spirituality in each other. And know that a strong faith will help sustain you in difficult times.
3. Shared core values are important. For instance, you can't have one person strongly believe in the value of discipline, as was true in Estelle's home, and one person living a life of disorganization.
4. Young or immature marriages often have unrealistic expectations. Be realistic in your expectations. "Don't expect more than each other can realistically give." And don't expect your marriage to be "all peaches and cream." Bad times come, and you can survive them.
5. Work on enhancing the good parts of your relationship. Take time for vacations and spend time together.
6. Be happy for the love and companionship you have.
7. You have to want to be in the relationship. You have to be with a man who also wants to be in the relationship.
8. Value your family and the support you receive and give.
9. Don't close yourself off. When a relationship ends, regardless of the reason, be open and willing to enter into another. You don't want to miss out on a good, long-term relationship.
10. You have to know your spouse to understand his tolerance levels, and you have to be patient.

Roses that have seen more seasons
tend to have
the sweetest scent.

Make time
every day
to smell them.

Chapter • Ten

Elizabeth

Elizabeth, the youngest of three children, grew up in Texas and New Orleans in the '50s and '60s. Her brother was three years older, and her sister was two years older. Her father's sister was an important figure who lived with the family during Elizabeth's last year in high school.

Her mom had a degree from Tulane business school and was one of only two women in the graduating class that year. An amazing accomplishment in the 1930s! Elizabeth's father had no college education.

Her parents' marriage was wonderfully atypical. In fact, Elizabeth characterized the marriage as an "unusually equal" one for that time. Her mother married at twenty-three and did not have any children until age thirty.

When Elizabeth was ten-years-old, her mother went to work in her father's plastic factory. Her dad was the president and ran the manufacturing and sales at the plant. As the vice president of finance, her mom handled all of the plant's money issues. In fact, her mother handled all things financial, both at the office and at home, including paying all the bills and giving her father a weekly allowance of ten dollars. On Fridays, which was payday, her dad, with check in hand, would knock on the door to their home and ask coyly if he could come in. Immediately upon entering, he would lovingly hand the check to his wife. (WHAT a perfect husband!)

Elizabeth remembers one time when her mom sent her dad to the bank to ask for a loan for the factory. When the loan officer asked him what his salary was, he took a wild guess because he really had no idea. When he relayed the story to the family later that day, mom laughed and agreed to give him a nice raise for taking care of the loan.

They were not only married to each other, they were also business partners and best friends. And they lived with a sense of humor. When they sold the business years later, her mom said "I guess we can't have any more board meetings in bed!"

The business was a family affair with Elizabeth working in the plant office during summer vacations. Although she really disliked the office work, Elizabeth valued seeing the business side of her mother. Elizabeth could easily see that her family wasn't the norm and that in most families the mother's sole role was to be the homemaker. Her mother was fortunate that her husband had a business that could benefit from her knowledge.

Her mother was primarily responsible for caring for the children. Her work presented absolutely no strain on the family. She was more than competent in both. In fact, Elizabeth easily says, "She was an awesome mother."

Elizabeth saw her father as a man who utterly adored his wife and "thought she was beautiful, inside and out." Her dad was very proud of his wife and never put her down in any way. (YEP. The perfect husband!) Elizabeth's mother realized that her husband was always going to do things his way. She was tolerant and sometimes sacrificed her own desires and opinions. The result was that Elizabeth's parents never argued. Elizabeth sees her mom as acquiescent, and her favorite aunt used to admonish her brother and his wife, saying that they were giving their children a totally unrealistic view of marriage. Today Elizabeth agrees wholeheartedly with her aunt's assessment.

As a child, Elizabeth wanted marriage and a family. In fact, Elizabeth wanted a marriage with many, but not all, of the traits of her parents' marriage. She wanted the adoration and respect of her parents' marriage, but she vowed to have more open and frank communication.

Her personal goal as a role model for her children was different. Elizabeth wanted her children to see that disagreements between a husband and wife are inevitable; she wanted them to realize that both husband and wife should express their opinions freely. Elizabeth wanted her children to know that it was okay and very normal for a couple to have disagreements. She wanted them to see that while spouses can feel strongly about their positions, disagreements need not escalate to quarrels. Elizabeth worked to instill in her children an understanding that disagreements do not "take the love away." To this day thanks to her upbringing, Elizabeth is not a fan of arguing, but she practices the old adage "don't suffer in silence." She advises you to always stick up for yourself.

Elizabeth credits her mother with being her strongest role model and was very proud of her. She also adored her aunt who showed a more conciliatory side. Although she didn't know her grandmother very well, she saw her as very strong willed. During her childhood, these women who were closest to Elizabeth were always able to maintain their identity. They never lost their strong sense of self.

Elizabeth attended college in the late 60s and was truly a child of the 60s, attending demonstrations and sit ins. In retrospect, Elizabeth describes her inner self in those years as "part feminist, part family." In other words, although her feminist side was very spirited, Elizabeth knew that her heart was anticipating a happy marriage with children. She knew her marriage would emulate the equality and mutual respect that her own parents had so clearly lived.

Although they met in high school, Elizabeth and her husband did not date until graduate school. Elizabeth attended graduate school in Austin, and he attended graduate school in Boston. Their long-distance relationship had some tensions, and they argued quite a bit during the courtship stage. Elizabeth found this somewhat unsettling as her wedding day approached. They were going to have to work to achieve Elizabeth's ideal of disagreeing without bickering.

She had dated a lot of different men, including at least one who did not know how to give in a relationship. She had enough experience to know that her betrothed was a good man, but the night before her wedding she remembers being thankful for being a Jew because "It is legal to get a divorce under Jewish law." She knew, however, that she wanted kids, and she wanted them with this man.

"I was a feminist of sorts but not very confident. I completed my master's and was working on my doctorate when my husband 'rescued me.' I was burned out and not very interested in completing the program. Today, I would tell you that I might have completed it, if they had had word processing at the time. It took endless retyping." When Elizabeth was halfway thru her doctorate, she happily welcomed the diversion her fiancé and marriage presented.

After their long-distance courtship, they married and moved to Philadelphia. She was twenty-seven and her new husband, Frank, was twenty-eight. The first of three children arrived two and a half years later.

Elizabeth had a master's degree and experience as a teaching assistant but didn't know what to do career wise. "He [her husband] encouraged me to pick up the phone and call colleges in the area. What a ridiculous thing to do in the middle of September! So I called the Community College of Philadelphia, and they said, "How soon can you come in?" One of the sociology professors had just come down with hepatitis. My lucky day," she says tongue in cheek. "Therein came my first real teaching job."

Elizabeth's next teaching position was one of note. Elizabeth taught a class on sex roles at Villanova. Here was a nice Jewish girl teaching about sex at a Catholic college while raising two young children and "railing against Barbie dolls and dresses." She was undoubtedly Villanova's most flaming feminist. What a wonderful experience for her students!

During this period Frank was working at the University of Pennsylvania. "For the first four or five years, he came home regularly at 6:00 P.M. We were very close. We tended to do everything together. Then his boss left, and Frank became acting VP. He now routinely came home at 10:00 P.M. I felt like our relationship had been severed. I was very frustrated and didn't know what to do. One night I faced it head on and told myself, I can either leave or find a way to make this work. I knew I didn't want to leave, so I determined that I needed to create a life for myself and find ways to get my needs for enjoyment and mental stimulation met. And that is what I did. At first, I found it sad. Like something died. But now I can't even remember what that would have felt like. I feel we are very close, but we have both shared and separate interests. We also share the *other person's* interests to some extent. I will go to some sports events with him, and he will attend some art exhibits with me. Part of my personal development was studying art appreciation at the Barnes Foundation for several years." Elizabeth hit a difficult time and vowed to take control and create something better. Personal development was a fabulous strategy. "I was able to do something constructive out of my unhappiness."

Elizabeth taught for a total of nine years – the latter part at Villanova in adjunct instructor roles. She left teaching when her third child was born, and her husband's career launched him into a hectic schedule of commuting to Boston every week.

Raising three children, taking care of the home, and having a busy professional husband who was often traveling was not Elizabeth's idea of what she wanted to do with her life. It was a very difficult time, when Elizabeth feels she lost touch totally with her most important component—her essence. Here was the feminist who had phenomenal role models within her very own family, suddenly feeling as though she had lost touch with her heritage and who she really was. She was taking care of three young children while her husband was flourishing in his career. Moreover, the marriage wasn't entirely as she had hoped or intended it to be. Bogged down in mundane household duties, Elizabeth felt frustrated and confused about where her life was going.

Elizabeth hit something similar to the saturation point we saw in Maureen's first marriage. Like Maureen, she was caught in an emotional whirlwind and was confused by her uncertainty about her identity and her life's path. She vowed to return to work when the time was right. In the meantime and after much self-assessment, she continued to cope with the chores and loss of self that rearing of young children often entails. During this difficult time as in every time of trial, Elizabeth had a strong sense of "we need to make it work."

When her youngest started school, Elizabeth returned to the job market as a temporary administrative assistant. "When that job ended, my husband told me that he did not want me taking anymore secretarial roles [because] it was a waste of my talents. After some floundering, I met with his former career counselor and his company ended up hiring me to work with people in transition."

"The day I got the job, I sent him a card. I have always mailed cards to my husband telling him that I love him. And thanked him for pushing me to reach my potential. I thought this job was such a perfect fit for me, and I couldn't believe they would actually pay me to do it!"

From her personal experience, Elizabeth believes that an indication of a good relationship is when both people are better because of the relationship and not worse. "My husband has encouraged me to grow, just as he has encouraged our children. I do believe that he has made me a better person. I hope I have done the same for him."

Being a professional career coach, Elizabeth has a thorough understanding of the Myer Briggs personality assessment. She and her husband have very different Myers Briggs results. This means that they each see the world very differently from one another.

One poignant and funny example of their strong individual differences is this wonderful story:

"I have three children, who are grown and on their own, for which I am very grateful. My oldest had learning and some physical challenges from a young age, and we were getting help at Children's Hospital since he was three. (He is now grown, married with a beautiful one-year-old son, and has a great job in DC).

At the age of five, he developed internal bleeding and ended up in the hospital. He was diagnosed with inflammatory bowel disease, which could be colitis, but they were not sure. At that time, which was about twenty-five years ago, it was thought that stress was a factor. So, during his stay at the hospital, my husband and I were asked to have separate interviews with a staff member, a psychiatric social worker, or psychologist. I assumed it was to see if we were the cause of this stress-related disease. One of the questions the person asked each of us was, "If you could have one wish granted for anything in the world, what would it be?" When my husband and I got back together, we compared answers. He said his wish was for peace in the world. Mine was a little more practical—a full-time maid!"

It is hard to imagine any two people having a greater polar opposite outlook on life!

Their children have benefited from these differences. In fact, raising their three children is a tie between Elizabeth and her husband that exemplifies qualities of a strong marriage. Despite their polar opposite attitudes, they have strong shared core values about child rearing, and in the words of Dinah, they ying - yang each other perfectly. For instance, Elizabeth's husband will push the children but Elizabeth does not. Elizabeth's husband encouraged the children to expand their horizons in all things, including school and he "pushed them out of the nest." Elizabeth simply communicated the importance of school. They are a perfect point counterpoint to one another.

Their children were taught early that to have money, you must earn it. Both Elizabeth and her husband believe that this understanding will create productive and confident adults, the ultimate goal of parenthood. They loved giving their children their bar mitzvahs and bat mitzvah, but instead of a spectacular party at a ritzy location, they toned things down quite a bit for each of these events. One of the themes was western and the teens wore flannel shirts and jeans. Elizabeth and Frank believe that rites of passage (both the Jewish celebrations and the high school and college graduations) are all about the children—not the parents. At the end of the special day's events, she and her husband were able to say, "We have accomplished this together."

If you ask Elizabeth what she feels are her strongest characteristics as a wife, she quickly answers with some significant attributes. The answer comes with ease because she is so in touch with who she is today. She's moved far beyond her emotional meltdown in the early years of their marriage. She is primarily a nurturer and is nurturing in all aspects of her life, including professionally as she continues to guide those in transition. Elizabeth is especially nurturing in her roles as wife and mother.

Elizabeth credits the longevity and happiness of her marriage with the good fortune of simply having "married the right person." She and Frank are committed to the marriage and are willing to compromise. Elizabeth's wisdom tells her that compromise often doesn't work if you married the wrong person. Their marriage is clearly one of mutual appreciation and respect. They might disagree, but they never put the other person down for his or her opinion. (Sure reminds me of Elizabeth's parents.) Each person is allowed and encouraged to use his or her individual strengths, and they pursue separate interests. Elizabeth is enormously supportive of Frank and says, "We both broaden each other's world." Their core values are the same, and both believe family always comes first. Jews from Texas, religion was a good foundation, but Elizabeth readily admits that she has always been more spiritual than Frank. The happiness in their marriage is fostered by fun, a good sense of humor, and a focus on important family issues. They have lived in the same house for thirty years despite the fact that finances could have easily warranted a "buying up." Status in homes and cars has never been paramount for either of them.

What is paramount, however, is having happy and healthy children who daily demonstrate the family's values. They are proud of how they raised unspoiled, confident children. To Elizabeth and Frank their happy, confident, loving and productive children are validations of their own success in life. "I love it when [Frank] adores our children and brags about them...He is close to the kids, and he is nurturing. He is smart, funny, caring, family oriented, and graduate of Wharton and Harvard. And most importantly, with us family always comes first!"

Her husband's heart attack twelve years ago was a challenging time. Elizabeth was scared but had a strong desire to "get him through this." Elizabeth says that the strengths you develop over life are the things that get you through. She had an unwavering commitment to the family and a robust confidence in herself. She tapped into her family for support, especially her sister. Her strongest role model, her mother, had illustrated a quiet strength that taught Elizabeth to get through each day, one day at a time, to educate yourself on the issues and to get help.

Elizabeth's desire is to nurture your rose garden with the following guidance:

1. Both you and your spouse should consider taking the Myers Briggs assessment. Contrast your results. This will give you quick insights into how differently you both look at the world, and may ultimately help you communicate better because you will understand each other more.

2. Does your marriage make both of you better people? If not, what can you do to change that? Does he bring out the best in you, and do you bring out the best in him? Does the best keep getting better? If so, congratulations! The long haul is yours for the taking! If not, take responsibility for finding ways to enhance who you are and who your spouse is. Perhaps that means taking a class together on a subject you both enjoy or perhaps it's going on that couple's retreat your church is offering or perhaps it is making a commitment to spend one weekend together per quarter. Take steps to make it better. Take those steps today.

3. Make sure you know how to compromise.

4. Keep your identity and communicate with your spouse if something doesn't strike you as fair or equal. Remember the lesson Elizabeth wanted her children to learn that disagreeing doesn't "take the love away." Talk with the intention of working it out. Whatever you do, "don't suffer in silence." But be fair and reasonable. You can be the peacemaker while making your position known.

5. Always have and show respect for one another.

6. Remember to say thank you to your spouse.

7. Foster a sense of humor in your daily lives.

8. Have fun! Don't allow yourselves to work too hard. Put your relationship on the top of the to-do list.

9. Create an environment in which each person is encouraged to use his or her strengths.

10. When tough times come, don't think of jumping ship too soon. Remember the cycle we discussed with Dinah, and see the early marriage difficulties of Elizabeth. Have patience, and believe that the best is yet to come.
11. Foster your own personal development as Elizabeth did by her studying art appreciation. You will be a happier person, and a happier person makes for a happier marriage.
12. Appreciate what you have. Take time to stop and reflect on the goodness that you have created. Acknowledge to your spouse the accomplishments you have attained, such as the graduation of a child or a new employment or business opportunity.

*The fruit of the rose, if allowed to develop,
has wondrous uses, including
skincare, soaps, decorations, cooking, beverages,
healing, perfumes, potpourri, and candles.*

Chapter • Eleven

Colleen

Colleen was born in 1957 and grew up in a happy, busy home in Worcester, Pennsylvania. She is the oldest of six children, five of whom are girls. Colleen's parents had five kids in six years. Seven years later they had another. Both her mother and her paternal grandmother were role models for Colleen. Her paternal grandmother had four children, as did her oldest daughter who became very ill and slipped into a coma after giving birth to her fourth child. After the daughter's death, Colleen's grandmother raised her daughter's children, showing Colleen the meaning of family, love, and nurturing.

Colleen's memories reflect a happy childhood. Her mom never worked outside the home. "She was beautiful, always dressed well, tall, narrow waist and small rear end, big bust, and blonde hair." Her mom was known for making goodies and for nurturing neighbors, friends, and members of her church. "She was beautiful and strong, the kind of woman that helped the neighbors." As was typical of her time, she also took good care of the children and the house. She was an outstanding cook, and every dinner included a yummy homemade dessert.

If Colleen's dad complained about anything around the house such as a messy room or dirty carpet, it would be totally taken care of by the time he got home at the end of the day. Money issues were never "Mom's thing." Bills and the checkbook were her dad's responsibility.

Today Colleen marvels that her mom was able to maintain daily harmony in the home with six children. And she knows that her parents really liked each other. "As far as I could tell, they never fought. It wasn't until I got older that I realized they didn't talk when they were fighting." Her parents have been married for over fifty years.

None of the women in her mom's social group worked, and no one ever got divorced except for Colleen's godmother. Her godmother was her mother's only sister, and she and Colleen were very close. Colleen attended Catholic elementary school for eight years. Her soul was saturated with a fear of God. As a young and impressionable Catholic schoolgirl, Colleen was worried sick that her beloved aunt and godmother would go to hell because she had divorced her husband. As a child, this fear caused her to lose sleep, but today she says, "The church has become much more ecumenical now."

Throughout her childhood, Colleen was certain she wanted to be a mom. She always wanted to be married and today believes that she was naïve to think she would be comfortable. "You want to give your children more than you had, but we didn't take the vacations that my [family took]. My parents were affluent. Dad worked a lot. He owned a tire business."

Colleen and her husband started dating when Colleen was only fourteen-years-old. By this time she was attending the local public junior high. They married when Colleen was twenty, and she got pregnant on her honeymoon.

Her pregnancy was difficult. During the fifth month, she developed preeclampsia, which forced the early delivery of her daughter. "I didn't think I would ever do it again. It was a terrible experience." Five years later Colleen relived the trauma, developing preeclampsia in her eighth month. This time she was seriously ill. "I was in misery. I didn't care if I died. Just get him out me!"

Colleen is trained as a hairdresser but only occasionally worked in this field. During the majority of her working years, she was a merchandising manager, buying the furniture and maintaining the inventory, for a high-end, privately owned furniture store. Recently she embarked on a new career in financial services.

When she was twenty-two and her husband was only twenty-three, he suffered from his first significant bout of depression, which the medical community then termed a nervous breakdown. Her husband's depression has waxed and waned over the years. When he is deeply depressed, Colleen takes control and ensures that her husband receives the care he needs. She is the family stronghold and leader when her husband is down and out and in need of intervention. Often this requires help from other family and professionals. Medication, therapy, hospitalization and intensive programs have been needed.

"I thought my marriage would be like my mom and dad's—get married, have kids, and no working outside the home. I am almost embarrassed to say it, but that was my expectation. I work and my husband doesn't. I am...Type A...always have to be doing something. My mom and dad would go out every Saturday night because my dad had clients. My husband doesn't enjoy going out, so we rarely do. He will always come up with some reason, so I go alone. I wish it was different."

Colleen and her husband had another big problem. When she was fifteen, their daughter was diagnosed with a rare blood disorder. She was born with this disease, but it was not discovered until she became very sick. She missed two years of high school because she had five hospitalizations and two major surgeries. "Her red blood cells aren't shaped properly. She had to have her gall bladder out. Then her spleen enlarged from being so busy breaking down red blood cells. She can't get exposed to certain viruses because they can kill her," Colleen explains.

When she was twenty, this daughter met a man who was out on work release. She conceived her first child three months later and brought the baby home to live with her and her parents. Colleen took it upon herself to provide for the newborn. "I was the one who got up every four hours for [her] asthma."

At the ten-year mark her daughter moved out and commenced a completely new life without her family. She gave full time custody of Samantha, her daughter, to Samantha's father. Colleen, her husband, and her granddaughter were heartbroken. "She didn't want to live with him. She wanted to stay with us."

Colleen and her husband were not even allowed to have her every other weekend. They went months being unable to see or speak with her. Christmas was especially heart-wrenching. "We didn't see her over Christmas. We didn't celebrate at all. First time I didn't have a tree." Colleen muses, "I never met anybody who had to give up a child and what that feels like."

Colleen and her husband were allowed only one visit in two years. Not only did they have the pain of knowing their granddaughter was unhappy, but they had to face that this pain was given to them by their very own daughter.

After two agonizing years without their grandchild, Samantha's father miraculously gave permission for his daughter to live with Colleen and her husband again in order to attend school in their school district. Colleen laughs lightheartedly when she mentions that as a child she had always imagined having three children. She had always wanted *at least* three kids. "We are now raising our granddaughter. She is twelve. God has a sense of humor!"

When I ask Colleen to what does she attribute the longevity of her marriage she responded, "Vows are a big reason." She remembers back to her childhood when her brother suffered with asthma. For his treatment, they used oxygen tents. "My mom and dad stayed together through that." Just like her parents before her, Colleen is clear, "For me, I took a vow when I got married. I said the words, *in sickness and in health*." She also emphasizes that "morally and spiritually, we are on the same page." While he is not today a practicing Catholic, he did convert to Catholicism before they married. Colleen says he did this because of his own desire. "I don't think you can force your views on another person. Your relationship with God is so personal." They both have a strong faith, and they pray. "The fact that this child is with us is a miracle. He feels the same way I do." They have unwavering life tested spiritual values and beliefs.

They also have a strong partnership despite her husband's serious challenges with depression. He makes sure there is food on the table, and he stresses a nutritious diet for Samantha. He takes care of the house and although Colleen will tell you it isn't always up to her standards, she is enormously appreciative of what he accomplishes. "I don't have the time or the energy."

In fact, Colleen and her husband have a long-standing partnership despite all the difficulties they have encountered. "We talk and support each other." Colleen emphasizes that the only other person who lost a child in the same way she did was her husband. Situations helped them to forge a tight bond. The day their granddaughter was removed from their home, together they went to a quiet and peaceful house owned by Colleen's sister on a lake. Together they sought whatever consolation they could find from nature and each other. They have also experienced the illness of their daughter, and what seems to Colleen to be a form of abandonment by their daughter as well. They can't find any answers as to why her daughter voluntarily vanished from their lives, but together they share the pain.

Colleen relishes certain aspects of her relationship with her husband. "I can talk with him about it, cry, and we can rejoice together." She can easily acknowledge how considerate he is. "He taught me generosity. He taught me how to be more giving. He is very kind, even when he is not well. When he is really in a bad way, nothing gets done, but he will still get Samantha to school, a half hour each way…four times a day. He is the one in the marriage who will send birthday cards. He would give you the shirt off his back, then his pants, and his shoes, too, even when he is not well."

Another strong reason for the duration of their marriage dates back to Colleen's most impressionable years. "I never wanted children by more than one man. I never wanted my children to have to live with a man who wasn't their father because of my aunt...My aunt's situation made such an impact...She had two girls and married again and had another child and a good marriage. He (the second husband) was good to the girls. It wasn't a bad situation at all. The impact was so great, more than I ever realized. Those ideas were so strong in me." The concern over her aunt's divorce haunts Colleen even in adulthood.

Today, Colleen will tell you something wonderful about her marriage of thirty-three years. "There is a lot of good. Now we have Samantha to raise! I can't do it alone while working fifty hours a week. She needs that love and comfort from him too... especially after all she has been through."

Colleen's ground rules for your rose garden:
1. Be considerate and respectful of one another no matter what the difficulty.
2. Despite everything that you go through, find the good that the other brings to the table, and the good your spouse creates in your family.
3. Develop and foster shared values through communication. Allow your experiences, both the good and the bad, to draw you closer together.
4. "Divorce is not in our vocabulary and is not an option. Think about that before you get married. Think about your differences, the idiosyncrasies that make you angry." Of course, there are certain "deal breakers" such as infidelity and abuse. "There is a lot of benefit of knowing someone loves you. You can trust him." The long-term survival of the marriage often gives you the benefit of this.
5. Acknowledge your own ability to give and take pride in your accomplishments. No two families are completely alike, but every family needs contributing, loving members. Recognize the value your spouse brings, but be sure to recognize and cherish your own ability to provide your own special gifts to your marriage and to your family.

Don't be disappointed in the beginning.
Your rose garden may fall short
of your expectations
in the first blooming season.

Chapter • Twelve

Bella

Bella was born in 1957 and grew up in Brooklyn. Her father had emigrated from Italy, and her mother was a second generation Italian American. She has a sister who is four years younger. Extended family was *still* family, and her maternal grandmother lived with them. Other extended family members lived in Brooklyn and nearby New Jersey. Some family remained in Italy.

Bella's mother had loved her job as an executive secretary in Manhattan, but tradition dictated a different life immediately after marriage. "A man was head of household, but a mother turned his head! A wife was subservient but not submissive. [She was] a traditional homemaker, cook, mother, and she had to leave her job to be married and raise kids."

Bella would largely describe her parents' marriage as traditional but with some distinct originality. For instance, her mother married at thirty-one, which was well beyond the norm then, and dad was twenty-eight. As you might expect, Bella's grandmother was the matriarch of the family.

Bella put the neighborhood women who were not Italian under her surveillance. She wanted to see how women could be different from her own loving mother and revered grandmother. She wanted to know that there were other options available for her own adulthood.

Bella envisioned her future self as an independent, strong woman with an interesting and fulfilling career. This was a Herculean but not impossible goal for a good girl from a large traditional Italian family. "I did not want any part of marriage," but everyone, especially family and other Italians, always wanted to know when she was going to get married.

Bella went away to college, and in traditional Italian style, returned home after graduation. At twenty-three, she thought she might get married, but the young man in whom she had a strong interest ended their relationship. His departure brought with it a lack of interest in any more romance, at least for a while.

At the age of twenty-eight, Bella convinced her family that she would have to move out of the family home to take a job she really wanted. It just so happened that her dream job was 250 miles away! You see, outside of marriage, a job was the only excuse Bella could possibly use to become the independent woman she wanted to be. She seized the opportunity and moved away from home. It was a formidable plan, but ultimately her family understood that the job she wanted was nowhere near their loving home.

As you can see, Bella was gutsy. She moved away in pursuit of a career, skillfully excelled at her chosen career, and horror of all horrors, did not get married until she was forty-five. As we discussed before when chatting about Gina, maturity has very special gifts for newlyweds. "Since I waited until forty-five to get married, my husband and I both entered into the marriage as independent, headstrong adults with equal partnership!"

But at age forty-five, sharing your home is not always an easy thing to do. (I have heard this from many women who lived alone and married later in life.) Bella was accustomed to her independence and her space. It took a concentrated effort and strategic planning to create a new environment in Bella's spacious condo where they both could have a solitary place when they wanted it. Neither one wanted to feel cramped with their new lifestyle.

Today, Bella will tell you that adapting to the married lifestyle was all about personal growth. "It took me a year to adjust to moving from [being] a single woman for forty-five years, to a wife largely because I wasn't used to compromising and what that meant. I learned not to sweat the small stuff like changing the color of my towels because my husband hated turquoise and instead focus on the big stuff. I found the process to be really uncomfortable, but looking back, it was one of the biggest learning experiences and made me more flexible and less rigid."

To both Bella and her husband, the first year of their marriage was like an amateur science experiment; there were times when Bella thought the intensifying pressure would cause the home lab to explode. Together they opted to hang in there. Now fifty-three, Bella continues her demanding consulting career and has successfully completed eight years of a wonderfully happy and fulfilling marriage!

While it might seem that she broke out of the traditional mindset, Bella will be the first to acknowledge that she hasn't completely escaped the expectations of her heritage. Every once in a while Bella is nagged by the thought that she should be more like her mother and cook more, keep a better home, and generally be the perfect wife. However, Bella remains convinced that her main role is to be caring not caretaking. "I have his back. I share his good days and bad days. But, I try not to lose myself in the relationship."

Bella says that happiness in a marriage is the result of realistic expectations, open communication, strongly shared values, an ongoing sense of humor, intimacy, and vacations! (Bella relayed this list to me while basking in the thought of their upcoming vacation to....guess where? If you guessed Italy, I am tapping my naso! Tombola!)

They use humor throughout the day and especially to break the tension whenever there is an argument. "When we really get mad at each other, one of us will ultimately crack a joke, and it frees us to get off our position and compromise."

"I do not look to my husband to define me, make me happy, or meet all of my needs. By enjoying our time together, I am happy in my marriage most of the time. We abide by spiritual principles but do not go to church. Do unto others as you would have them do unto you is our motto."

Bella is wise. She knows how to identify and remember special moments that many of us would consider ordinary. Bella knows that if you really listen to your spouse, what might appear to be an ordinary moment can be a special gift to be cherished. "[H]e called me out of the blue one day and told me how much he appreciated me and loved me, and how glad he was that we were married. That spontaneous show of affection was amazing!"

Bella also fondly remembers the words of a close friend describing her thoughts on the worse days of her own marriage. "There are 100 reasons to leave, but 101 reasons to stay." In a good marriage like Bella's, there are always more reasons to stay than to leave. Bella values every one of them no matter how seemingly small or subtle.

Advice from Bella's sunny rooftop garden:

1. "Love changes form and shape," not unlike the rose bushes in your garden. Expect change and use it to foster your personal growth and the growth of your relationship.
2. Watch for and appreciate the not-so-ordinary ordinary moments.
3. Don't compare your love to others. No good can come from this. Ever.
4. Be true to yourself. Know who you are. Be confident that you can take care of yourself *no matter what.*
5. Be patient and wait for the dust to settle when your marriage is experiencing a bit of a kerfuffle such as the painful adjustments Bella and her new husband experienced when they first started living together.
6. Allow your spouse to love you. (There HAS to be a story here, Bella.)
7. Laugh at yourself and laugh together. Every day.
8. Maintain and foster your friendships. These relationships will enhance your life. Your friends will be there for you as strengtheners whenever the tough times come.
9. While you might not be interested in riding a two legged, rabid camel through the Sahara, definitely take stimulating vacations. Time spent together creating new exciting experiences and memories will enhance your relationship beyond words! (If you can't agree on where to go, what oh what should you do? How about a...um...a...*compromise?* Maybe you pick this year's trip and your husband can pick next year's. But allocate a couple of extra budgeted dollars for his trip since he has to wait. Remember to be the peacemaker.)
10. Make sure you both really want to be in the relationship. It will get you through the trying times, and will make all the effort worthwhile.

The Hildesheim Rose,
a legendary rose 1,000 years old,
climbs in the apse of the medieval St. Mary's
Cathedral in Hildeseheim, Germany.
Allied bombs destroyed the cathedral in 1945.
The rosebush survived thanks to strong roots
deep below the surface.

Chapter • Thirteen

Liv

Liv grew up during the 1950s on a farm near Adams, Minnesota, a very small town that dubs itself the "Pride of the Prairie"; she was the youngest of five children in a solid clan that focused on hard work, God, and family. "My parents came from large families, so there were lots of cousins in the area and good family memories. I grew up with one set of grandparents. The other set had already passed away. I was born when my mother was forty-two, and my dad was thirty-four. My father was a farmer, and my mother was a teacher. (I am having déjà vu.) Raising five kids was probably no picnic, but they never let on."

The farm life was as traditional as apple pie, heterosexual marriage, and square dancing. (Did you know that nineteen states have named the square dance as their official state dance?) Her mom gave up teaching when she married. "She had five children in ten years. Ouch. She was energetic, a good cook, and fun but serious as well. She supported my dad's business of farming. She had a lot of say in what went on, but he had final say—pretty traditional for a Midwestern Lutheran marriage. She was very busy with domestic chores and supporting the family, so we did not have many quality discussions because she was busy. I always knew she was there for me, however."

Liv's Scandinavian heritage taught her that issues were not talked about openly. Rather you keep to yourself on important subjects. "I found that I could speak to friends about issues more [easily] than my parents. One thing I did appreciate was that my parents did not argue or have conflict in front of their kids. In retrospect, I like that model, especially when kids are younger and don't know how to process parental conflict."

Growing up, Liv's concept of marriage was that it was just something everybody does. The role of the woman was to support the husband and the children. A college graduate, Liv married in her mid-thirties and a beautiful baby boy arrived a few years later. She assumed that her husband was a person she could be friends with forever, depend upon for financial parity, and whose company she would enjoy. "We liked many of the same things, so it seemed like we might have gone through the most difficult times working out our relationship for five years before we were married." Liv doesn't hesitate today to say that her expectations were not at all close to what actually came to pass.

Her husband, Dave, is Jewish and grew up in Brooklyn and Queens; he experienced intense sibling rivalry that was agitated by his mother's attitude. His brother excelled at everything he touched, attending college at the age of sixteen and becoming a successful entrepreneur by early adulthood. His mother was not hesitant to make sure Dave knew that he somehow was "always short of the mark."

When Liv would ask for help with normal family duties and chores, what Dave heard was his mother once again reinforcing his shortcomings. Dave was not capable of hearing *partner* in Liv's requests. He was only capable of perceiving that he was being found lacking. Liv realized somewhere in the therapy process that Dave saw some version of his mother in her. Both women loved fashion, always looked great, were extremely competent, and were successful in business.

Dave also grew up in a combative environment where the modus operandi was speaking over the other person loudly in order "to win." There was no real listening. In contrast, with the five children in Liv's home, they buried a lot within "Minnesota nice." While Dave could be fun, fresh, and open, fighting would supplant that best of their relationship. The fighting was far "dirtier" than Liv had ever experienced. This type of communication style makes conflict resolution difficult if not impossible without professional help.

Liv realized that if she remained in the marriage, she could live with her head in the sand, or she could be straightforward. She opted for the latter strategy, and told Dave that she could not possibly continue to live in a contentious environment; she reminded him that she was his wife—not his mother. Liv was also concerned that their son was adversely affected by the vehement arguing. Dave believed it would toughen him up, but Liv believes it is important to show children how to be civil while working toward a resolution to a conflict. "I am an adult, and I can take it," Liv said, "but my kid isn't going to." Dave came from an environment were open conflict was the norm, and he seemed to thrive on it. Live found it hard to tolerate. "I ultimately drew a line in the sand…and made [contentious showdowns] a marriage deal breaker. He got it. It also became better for me, not just my son. It does not mean we do not fight, but it is done differently and not always in an open forum." Liv's decision to be honest about her feelings helped Dave gain a greater understanding of their differences, and a greater respect for Liv and their relationship. In the end, the situation vastly improved.

One day Dave quit his job to find himself. "He did not discuss it with me but told me afterward. We had a two-year-old at the time. You fill in the blanks …" He had no plan, and she was quite understandably angry. By far, it was one of the biggest trials of their marriage, and at the time, she couldn't visualize their marriage continuing because the deep strain caused them to grow apart, and Liv's travel schedule made it easy for them to live parallel lives. "I pursued therapy and lots of discussions with friends and siblings about my situation and …my husband's career decisions. I was too angry to engage much with my husband, so sought other sources of support." Liv knew her inner core well and realized "that I was able to make it on my own, which is what it felt like, and it ultimately came down to my determination to keep things going financially."

Her husband eventually became involved with a start-up company that didn't involve any money at first and subsequently resulted in partner riffs and stresses. Liv was angry for a long time at her husband, and spent a long time in therapy trying to sort things out. She resented being left "holding the bag." It wasn't easy, but Liv eventually forgave her husband when she realized that he wasn't emotionally equipped to handle the stresses of corporate America. She knew that she excelled in a corporate environment and that she and Dave could complement each other's strengths and weaknesses. Over the years, they have grown closer.

"My husband is spiritual but not religious. I am spiritual but ascribe to more traditional religious practices. He is Jewish, and I am Christian. He comes to church with me from time to time to show spiritual connectedness. I think that is a nice contribution from him. He did not have strong feelings about continuing Jewish traditions for our son. As a result, our son was raised in a Presbyterian setting and goes to church—less now that he is a sixteen-year-old. He is also a spiritual soul. We all pray individually and as a family not only at meal time, but as an avenue to approach life's joys and challenges giving us all greater perspective beyond oneself."

Three and a half years ago, Liv suffered a neuropathic pain disorder called burning mouth syndrome. Diagnosis was difficult because the syndrome is rare. It felt as though there was scalding water in her mouth. The pain can escalate to the point where it feels as though her tongue and gums are actually on fire. It can last for years but can be manageable with proper treatment and the realization that some days are better than others. "It took me several months to get a diagnosis, and then I had to find someone who would not think I was crazy, but try to help me with pain management."

Early in her illness, she saw that her husband was nicer to her; he seemed to like her more and feel less threatened. Liv both liked and disliked Dave for this. You see, marriage, even for strong women, is not a black and white thing. Shades of gray exist almost every day. Liv, however, is very appreciative of her husband's help. "My husband has been very supportive through this time. My syndrome has improved a bit, but there are days, when the pain is greater, that I do not function well. He has been as helpful as he can. He tried to help with research and has been there for me to try to manage the pain and associated lifestyle adjustments. It meant that I was not alone. I felt supported through a difficult time."

Liv will tell you that marriage is a process. "You realize that you are two very different people and that you try to support each other's strengths and weaknesses."

She believes it is imperative for a woman not to lose herself to her marriage. Liv described her friend from high school, Olivia, who is currently in her third marriage. In each marriage, Liv has seen Olivia mirror her husband's interests. For Liv, it is not the number of marriages of her friend, but rather the seeming loss of the inner core of her friend to a husband's persona. And Liv can't talk to her as much anymore because her husband does not like her to be on the phone when he is around. Liv always maintained her individuality. It has been important to her to keep her soul and some independence intact within her marriage.

Liv and her husband believe in a partnership and in compromise. The fact that Liv has always traveled extensively for work didn't allow her to lose herself in her marriage or family life. She did work hard to be home for school events and birthdays and also made sure to have an honest, hard-working college student to help around the house, particularly when both she and Dave were traveling.

She has survived significant problems in her marriage and the tiresome, back-stabbing, and male-dominated culture of financial services. Liv has thought about not working, but the thoughts of not working frightened her more than the temptation to write, to volunteer, to cook can overcome. She sees herself as the person who is needed to provide the raw ingredients for the family soup and that means going to work and making her sales numbers every month.

Liv is very happy about the personal development she has experienced during these married years. She takes time for her female friendships and for special weekends at personal growth seminars and events.

She unequivocally puts the survival of her marriage down to the decision that having two parents under one roof would be best for her son. "That was the decisive factor in staying in my marriage through twenty years. I eventually saw good balancing traits to my personality as well. I think that having a child makes you stop and think about the randomness of leaving when conflict arises. My husband's job changed, and he decided to find himself in his early forties by looking for a new career. This completely skewed my perception of provider/father/husband. I became main provider and [was] not sure I liked the role. It needed to be done, and I had to make a choice to step into that role."

What makes a happy marriage according to Liv is contentment, a low level of regular conflict, and intimacy to smooth out the rough spots.

Of the women with whom I spoke, Liv was alone in advising that you consider how you were raised and how your prospective spouse was raised. Look long and hard at his relationship with his mother. If he was raised very differently than you, beware or think that through. Furthermore, you may end up comparing your husband to your dad or your brothers, especially if those were positive role models for you. If the match isn't as close from a value perspective, you begin to wish for those values in your man and your marriage. Values need to be similar, and if you were raised differently, conflicting ideas might arise later in the marriage.

Her therapy taught her that life is never perfect and that issues come and go throughout life. She could love her husband, but might not always like him. Liv said, "I can give up some of my personal happiness and…see how this goes." Her closest friends have told her she is "too adaptive" in many areas of her life. But her ability to adapt is what has given both her always evolving marriage and her stressful career their longevity. Liv has successfully weathered blows in her marriage and her career by working hard to assess her options and determine the path she wants to follow.

Today, it is safe to say that Liv is glad she made the choice to stay in the marriage. She believes that she and her husband are a good team and that their son, now a junior in high school, is a person they can be proud of. She realizes, however, that when he goes off to college, new challenges may arise, and she will be ready to deal with them when they do. She always is and she always will be.

Like the Hildesheim Rose, your garden will need some strong, deep roots to survive any unanticipated allied bombing.

1. Make sure you understand your past AND your husband's. Liv cautions you to take a full inventory of your man's background. You really have to figure out what makes him tick in order to communicate well and have a happy, well-functioning home environment. Understand his relationships with the women throughout his life, including past girlfriends but most especially his mother.

2. You also need to foster fun in your relationship. It will help you leave the serious stuff aside sometimes and enhance the relationship.

3. While Liv worked hard to change Dave's communication style to one she knew she could deal with, she wants you to know that it is never a good idea to assume that you can change your spouse. Her parents' solid relationship and good communication skills were Liv's prototype, but not all of us have the benefit of such solid role models.

4. Know that when tough times arrive, you need to find the external help that best suits you and your situation. For Liv, intelligent and effective help came from a competent therapist who was able to guide Liv in seeing her situation clearly and also in identifying and implementing viable coping strategies.

5. Strong bonds with lifetime friends allow you to keep perspective and help shoulder the rough patches. Always maintain the friendships that are keepers and that provide support and allow you to have fun beyond your core relationship. Ask your closest friends or family members for their insight and support on big issues that you face – they know you and sometimes your spouse as well. It can help provide a more holistic view of your relationship.

6. Look for the good in one another and be willing to work to complement each other's strengths and weaknesses.
7. Realize that a marriage is a process and not a single day, argument, or disagreement. Be willing to work through the droughts, the infestations, and the allied bombings to get to the garden full of sweet-smelling blossoms.
8. Despite what you saw as a child in terms of conflict resolution, assess your options. Do you want to play ostrich and ignore what's happening or do you want to address the situation openly with your partner? If you choose the latter, your next step is to identify the ways you could initiate dialogue. Remember Sarah's peacemaker rule when you are deciding which option to pursue.

To keep your roses in front of your mind,
the guidelines for growing your roses
need to be revisited from time to time.

And your rose garden needs your care
regularly throughout the year,
even during the blooming seasons.

Chapter • Fourteen
Guidelines for Your Garden

No nonfiction book on wives and marriage would be complete without a chapter dedicated to advice. Within this chapter is a list of the gems compiled from many women, mostly from those you've just met.

If you are a newlywed or contemplating a commitment, you will want to take notes and use a highlighter on this chapter. If you are in an existing relationship, cull this chapter for new approaches to enhance your marriage and consider adding to our list by going to www.sothisishowitfeels.com.

If you are a mother (or a father!) and you are giving this book to your daughter because you want her to have a wonderful, long term and well-functioning marriage, how very nice!

If, however, you are a mother of the meddling variety (and sometimes that is just what we *must* be!) with perhaps well-meaning but not welcome intentions, don't highlight anything. Don't put any notes in the margin. In fact, don't even speak. Promise me you will say absolutely nothing. Just put this book in a pretty gift bag. In fact, you might even want to give it to your daughter (or future daughter-in-law) anonymously. If your daughter actually reads this book, perhaps you won't have to say "I **told** you so!" at some point in the future!

The Marriage Commitment

Guidance for the Long Haul

1. Have a **realistic** vision of your future together that includes **agreed upon expectations**. These words are the best: Get out of any fairy tale mentality. This is a no-win outlook. Be realistic. I can't word this concept any better than these words that were inspired from Gail and Leslie.

When all the stress and excitement of the engagement party, wedding shower, wedding, and honeymoon are behind you, what do you envision next? Can you imagine life and all its routines, and ups and downs with your partner? Seriously try to picture the future reality. Does it appeal to you? If not, perhaps you need to slow down the plans, talk, and reconsider.

Early in your thoughts about marriage, talk about whether you want children. Will your family practice a religion? What form will it take? Do you want a rural existence? How do you anticipate handling aging parents? Under what circumstances, if any, would divorce be a viable option? And in the wise words of twice-married Estelle, "Don't expect more than each other can realistically give."

2. If you plan on being **good communicators**, a 'must have' trait for your marriage to go the long haul, you should be communicating now. It is a daily exercise, not something you wait to do when a crisis occurs.

3. Make a resolution that you keep to **say I am sorry**. I was wrong.

4. Make plans together but **expect change**. It is inevitable. You need to be flexible and strong. No wimps should get married. If you are a wimp, consider a nunnery instead.

5. **Be honest with yourself**. When you begin to delude yourself with thoughts that you can change him or you'll learn

to love each other or he is not really lazy, you are on a very slip-pery slope and headed right off your garden plot. In fact, you have commenced on a path that will take you so far away from yourself that you won't know where to find **you**. You could wander in a parched desert for forty years never seeing a single rose.

6. Don't expect your marriage to be all passion and fun. For your garden to thrive, you must do more than smell the roses. You have to prune, and mulch, and water, and debug and on and on. You both are going to have to **"work" at it**.

7. Understand your husband's past and consider whether it will **mesh** well with your background. Communicate about how you envision your life together.

8. **Trust your instincts**. Some folks have very loud instincts that protect them from all kinds of problems. Other folks have teeny, tiny voices that they sometimes choose to ignore. If you hear so much as a whisper, stop and be honest with yourself. At a minimum, reread number five above.

9. It is not your job to change your spouse, and you should not make plans to do so. In the wise words of Liv, "It is never good to assume you can change your spouse." **Appreciate him for who he is,** and if you can't, well then…at a minimum consider counseling. You need to find out if you are the problem because if you are, you will try to fix the men in your subsequent rela-tionships. If he really does need to be fixed or if together your combination is toxic, I encourage you to plant another variety of rose.

10. Do you have **shared core values**? If not and if you are hell-bent on doing this thing called marriage anyway, you better be more flexible than my sweet determined dog, Harry. Harry can most gracefully Houdini himself out of a triple harness if he gets even a fleeting scent of another four-legged creature with whom he wants to rendezvous. There is a difference, however, between you and Harry. When Harry is so flexible that he gets out of his

harness and gets lost, he knows no remorse. Unless you are a bit crazy, you are not likely to be as lucky.

Do you get it? If you don't have shared core values like mutual respect, kindness, honesty, sincerity, family comes first, and loyalty, your flexibility will have to be so strong that you will violate rule number five by being completely dishonest with yourself.

11. Never define yourself by your relationship with your spouse. **Let YOU define** who you are and never let a relationship take the splendid **YOU** away. Enhancing your life with pursuits such as Elizabeth's art appreciation, Liv's seminars, and Jessie's spiritual courses and self-development programs is helpful.

12. Every day **laugh** with your spouse and laugh without him (preferably not with the other man— remember your shared core values young lady!) Be happy. It is contagious.

13. Always make time for sex. (I bet you wanted me to list this as number one!) **Good sex** fosters intimacy far beyond the physical.

However, I wouldn't try locking your young child out of the house to get privacy for sex. (You can totally trust me on this one.) Such a parenting strategy has some accompanying self-flagellation particularly if the neighbor's nasty Jack Russell manages to jump his fence into your yard, or if your deck's growing beehive is particularly active. Or perhaps your sweet little girl just happens to have a very small bladder and is banging on the bolted back door for an emergency potty visit. In any case, you don't want your future sex life ruined by guilt, not to mention the possible detrimental effect on both junior and your relations with your neighbors.

14. Know and maintain your key **strength supporters**. For Estelle, Gina, and many others like them, great sustainable strength comes in the form of prayer and faith in our Creator and the great plan of the universe. A common religion is a big strength for any marriage. If you are fortunate enough to have a common

religion, you should nurture spirituality in each other. And know that a strong faith will help sustain you in difficult times.

My friend and interviewee, Carol, tells me that she and her husband pursue their spirituality by being members of a local wine club! The probability of this club being spiritually supportive is debatable, but it certainly qualifies for extra points as it adheres to both rules nineteen and twenty-nine. Congrats to Carol and her husband! They hit two rules with one bottle!

For many of us, girlfriends who are there for the celebrations and the tough times are our strongholds. For others, like Liv, a great source of strength is a therapist. For many, open communication between spouses can serve as the best strength. Try cultivating an arsenal of resources on which to rely in tough times.

15. Don't be a pathetic, crying sap when it is over. Know that sometimes it is just time to move on. Do not let yourself look backward. Figure out your best options, make decisions, and press on to a better day. **Take positive action** toward your new life. There is more than one variety of rose. Go plant something else.

Most definitely do not give up on the institution itself. Think of all you have learned! If Maureen had given up after marriage number one, she and Scott would never have experienced the wonder that their current marriage gives them every day. If Leah had refused her third proposal, she would have missed the happiness that she, her son, and her husband currently share.

Your experiences have taught you so much that your next relationship or marriage will benefit from all you have learned. As you can see from the lives chronicled in this book, often second or even third marriages have many of the necessary ingredients for successful, happy marriages. Ignore the statistics! As my much-loved mother would always say, "**Pick yourself up, dust yourself off, and start all over again**."

16. Almost every wife talked about the need for **patience** in marriage. A wise rule of thumb is to temper any immediate

response when something untoward happens with a countdown: the more patience you think you might need, the higher the starting number. For example, when your husband dislikes the Julia Child dish that took you three hours to make, you should probably start the countdown at 500. So, on the night Liv's husband told her that he had quit his job, I think it would have been wise had she started her countdown at a very high number. Bazillion. Bazillion minus one. Bazillion minus two. Bazillion minus three—you get my drift.

17. There are going to be times when your spouse needs you. You may feel that the issue is not that serious or not worth cancelling a meeting or a girls' day at the spa. Do it anyway. If there is an issue and your spouse expressed a need for you to be there, do not trivialize the need. What your spouse is feeling about the issue is obviously different than what you are feeling. To be a spouse in a time-tested marriage, you have to **be there** for him, and he has to be there for you. It is the golden rule in a marriage. (I am assuming here that you are married to a grown up and not to someone who needs you to be home cooking chicken soup for every cold and hangnail. If my assumption here is incorrect, you married a wimp and violated rule number four.)

18. Both you and your spouse should consider taking the **Myers Briggs assessment**. You will understand each other better and communicate more effectively as a result. More than one marriage I examined for this book benefited from doing this. Work with a professional to understand your results.

19. Be sure to **make time for one another regularly**. In this day of constant pressures from work and family responsibilities, you can fall into the trap of taking your time together for granted. It's so easy to promise to make time after a business trip, the holidays, crunch time at work, etc. Realistically, if you don't make spending time together a priority, some other demand will

claim your attention, and your time with your spouse will slip down your to-do list. Plan a vacation together, and put it on the calendar. **Create new experiences** that you share.

One wife I interviewed is in a marriage where both spouses have numerous business commitments that regularly run into the night. They have a pact with each other that Wednesday nights are their night. Nothing can be planned for Wednesday, and there are no exceptions. This is a golden rule for their marriage, and it is working.[1]

20. Take time to **contemplate the good** you see in your spouse, and from time to time make sure you **communicate** your observations to your spouse. Consider establishing a **My Favorite Things** book similar to Maureen and Scott. Daily you will note in this book what your husband did that you really appreciated. He will do the same for you. Reciprocation is a key ingredient to make a marriage good. Both parties give and receive. Examples are

"My favorite thing today was your shoveling the driveway and walkway while I slept in."

"My favorite thing today is when you went grocery shopping."

"You made me laugh so hard I cried when you tied your yak-king mother up in the basement today!"

"My favorite thing today was when you washed our new RV and successfully expunged the skunks. I had no idea a mama skunk could have that many babies."

"My favorite thing today is when you offered to go to the wine and spirits store to replenish our Maneschevitz."

"My favorite thing today was when you didn't get upset when I washed your vintage 1969 Grateful Dead T-shirt with my red fuzzy robe. I am sorry. Seriously though, you really do look

---

1   More on this in *So This Is How It Feels to Be a Wife: The Next Dozen.*

good in pink." (FIVE points here! Saying I'm sorry counts for four!)

"Thank you for not saying anything when you were carving the turkey tonight and had to pull out the paper wrapper complete with all the organs. I didn't know they wrap up that stuff and put it in the empty cavity! Your new boss was very gracious, too."

"You were so amazing to my friend, Tasha, today. It took a lot to let her move in after the collapse of her fourth marriage. She says she won't stay as long as she did last time."

"Thank you for speeding the screeching cat to the vet today. I don't think Johnnie realized she was close enough to catch fire when he lit the match for the M80."

"I really appreciated your gently extracting the splinters from my behind today. I promise I won't need you to do that again."

All kidding aside, you can make these things as spicy as you would like but keep it true, and remember each spouse's job is to be sincere and to make sure you each do something notable daily that can be written in the journal.

If you don't want to do a daily journal, consider giving your spouse a **list of all the reasons you love and respect him** on your anniversary. On their twenty-second wedding anniversary, Dana, another woman I interviewed, gave her husband a list of twenty-two reasons why she loves and respects him. She carries the list with her every day on her cell phone, making it easy to add another reason when he does something particularly special. She will be all ready not only for their twenty-third anniversary but for their fiftieth and sixtieth anniversaries as well. By carrying the list close, she also can refresh her memory about all her husband's good qualities when he does something that she finds less than pleasing!

21. You need to **have your own career skills** even if you decide not to work. The rate of divorce is staggering, and every

woman should be able to take care of herself and her family if there is a problem. **Expect the unexpected** because something is bound to happen. Death, divorce, loss of employment, a downturn in your or your spouse's business could be disastrous. Your ability to provide for yourself will also reduce your fear should you need to find employment.

An added benefit is that you emotionally have more freedom to leave a relationship should you choose to do so. It is nice to know you remain in a relationship because of the relationship and not because of the fear of being unable to provide for yourself. I have seen this happen. We all probably have. It is not a pretty sight.

22. Have you shared a **laugh** with your husband today?

23. When devastation strikes, let the situation play out, feel your feelings, then **absolutely find the gift** from the adversity. Talk with your spouse, and share the gift from the difficulty together. This is one of my favorite garden rules! Thank you, Jessie. Be sure to **lean first on one another** when adversity arrives. (Remember Dinah.) **Allow your experiences, both the good and the bad, to draw you closer together.**

24. Realize that neither of you are perfect. Given that you have imperfections, realize that you are not always right. Let yourself **see your husband's perspective** as well. There is often not a "correct" answer. Sometimes a difference of opinion is simply a difference of legitimate and viable opinion. Remember to **be flexible** but hold your ground when you absolutely cannot live with a different solution. Make the latter situations few and far between. In other words, when an issue is not of paramount importance, **have the ability to give in.** In the familiar words of Sarah, "You don't want to kill each other over nothing."

Consideration for each other must be at the top of the list in every marriage. **Good communication** will require both parties to speak and both parties to listen. Give up the need to be right and **develop a need to communicate** instead! Train your teeny, tiny inner voice to shout out to you my favorite quote from Sarah, "**BE THE PEACEMAKER!**"

Insist on talking through problems, and **push for a resolution** that might require **compromise**. But always see yourself as a peacemaker.

Be sure to keep your identity and communicate if something isn't fair or equal. Remember **disagreeing doesn't "take the love away."** Talk with the intention of working it out. Whatever you do, "don't suffer in silence." Always be fair and reasonable. **Live the role of a peacemaker**.

25. Financial problems are believed to be the number-one stressor in marriages. **Be a proactive partner on financial issues**. Know what is going on and participate in bill paying, investment decisions, budgeting, and expenditures. Do not abdicate your role as partner when it comes to money because ignorance of important issues can hurt the family in an emergency and you could grow resentful of your spouse's role as sole guardian of the family finances.

26. Be judicious in how you involve your parents and your in-laws. Don't let their issues impact your home and your decisions.

27. Relationships with others are very important. **Maintain and foster strong friendships,** and encourage your spouse to do the same.

28. **Don't dwell on a problem**. In the words of Sarah's mother, "Don't wear your dirty laundry on your sleeve." And as Gina advised, don't bring up the problem again months later. (Because, remember, you pushed toward and found a resolution at that time, right?)

This rule goes hand in hand with fostering and maintaining a good attitude. In Sarah's wise phraseology, **expect your marriage to be good and then work to make it good**.

29. **Develop interests that are separate and distinct from your spouse's interests. Have common interests as well.** Dana was really good at this; her family stays close, no

matter what the latest disagreements might be, by regularly playing games or cards together. She and her husband expect to unite over games just as many families unite over dinner. It can have ice-breaking and unifying effects, similar to the unexpected joke in the middle of Bella's squabbles with her spouse.

30. **Anticipate your spouse's needs** in difficult situations and take the reins if at all possible. The appreciation this engenders is well worth all the effort.

31. **Make it a fundamental truth that neither party would ever do anything to hurt the other.** This idea from Maureen is another favorite of mine.

32. **Love each other's family** as much as you love your own. (That includes the meddling in-laws about whom we could write an entire book, but I am not going to. Despite what others may tell you, I am not that crazy).

33. Not only is a marriage a process, but also it is a **partnership.** Practically every wife I interviewed used the word *partnership* or described the concept. Revisit some of the women's stories, and you will see it showing through even if the word wasn't actually used.

The best attributes of a partnership showed when Dinah and James hit adversity. They took the normal daily partnership to a new level when they had their **ying - yang** thing through James's unemployment. They conducted their own intimate orchestra, and it worked. Replicate them. What a gift they developed together in partnership through a very tough time!

34. Don't assume that your marriage needs to be a fifty-fifty partnership for it to work. **Don't look for parity** in all things. If Maureen is correct, fifty-fifty marriages are a myth. (If you have a marriage that is a fifty-fifty partnership you can pass go and go straight to rule forty).

35. Look for the good in one another and be willing to work to **complement each other's strengths and weaknesses.**

36. Realize that a **marriage is a process** and not a single day, argument, or disagreement in time. **Be willing to work** through the seasons, the droughts, the infestations, the allied bombings to get to the garden full of sweet-smelling blossoms.

Does your marriage make both of you better people? If not, what steps can you take to change this? Be proactive.

37. **Know** what **your priorities** are and make sure a major priority is your relationship.

38. **Understand** each other's goals and talk about them. **Support each other's dreams and celebrate successes.**

39. And by the way, laugh at yourself. You are pretty funny.

40. **Appreciate what you have.** Take time to stop and reflect on the goodness that you have created. Acknowledge with your spouse the accomplishments you have attained, including a strong marriage, the graduation of a child, a new employment or business opportunity.

And watch for and **appreciate the not-so-ordinary ordinary moments.**

When times get tough, take the day you are living and make it worthwhile *with your spouse.* Forget about what your problems might do to your tomorrows, and **realize you have something worth celebrating every day**.

Your children will be able to talk about the great role models their parents were. How fabulous is that?

Conclusion

SO…you might be wondering if I figured out why my relationship (you know, the one I briefly mentioned in the preface) crashed and burned. You might be wondering if this project helped me identify the reasons my relationship failed. I am happy to say that the answer is an adamant YES.

First of all, we only communicated about the easy stuff. We didn't communicate about anything too difficult for us to face together. Instead, we kept important thoughts to ourselves and came to our own very private conclusions. He might argue this point with me, but he would be wrong. His last action, the disappearing act, proves my point.

Second of all, we never made a commitment for the long haul. We made a verbal commitment for monogamy for today and tomorrow, but we never agreed to speak any formal vows. If this isn't a sign, I don't know what is. In fact, in the words of one of my most mature girlfriends (who just so happens to call my ex-best bud, poopy head) "It was inevitable." Is she right? You bet she is.

Early on with this relationship, I made the decision that if things started to unravel, I would not work to reweave them again. I said to myself all along, "I will let this relationship play itself out." How could I ever have expected a different outcome when I was not willing to work on the relationship? I was not willing to commit, and I was not willing to work on it. How is that for, in the words of Jessie, "owning my own stuff?"

Can I break down more of the reasons? Identify what was right and more of what was wrong about the relationship? Sure. It is pretty easy to do that now. What matters is that I don't repeat the same mistakes next time.

I also know that poopy head left because he could feel better elsewhere. In his mind, he wanted to move to a place of better feelings for him. Who can fault that? Don't we all want to feel the best we possibly can? He and I had never made the commitment to "go the long haul." And I would never want to deny him the chance to feel better. I admire his ability to "go for it." I couldn't do it even though it was time.

For me, what really matters now is what I do with what I have learned from these thoughtful women who opened their private lives to you and to me.

This is my pledge, my contract with myself for my future.

I, Terri L. Smith, promise that I will take each piece of luminous, sound, and commonsense advice herein and make it my own. Thank you Sarah, Gail, Leslie, Maureen, Dinah, Gina, Leah, Jessie, Estelle, Elizabeth, Colleen, Bella, Liv, Carol, and Dana.

I will use your heartfelt wisdom to replenish my own promising garden.

Thank you from the bottom of my heart.

Signed: Terri L. Smith
       Terri L. Smith

You should formalize this promise to yourself, too.

I wish you the best blooming season ever, and remember to take time along your journey to stop and smell your roses.

About the Author

Terri L. Smith is an unemployed wealth-management banker who is basking in her free time. She used her skills of consulting with clients about all aspects of their finances to interview women of diverse ages and backgrounds for this book.

Terri has had one unsuccessful marriage and is quite happily divorced. In the words of Elizabeth, Terri quite simply "married the wrong man." But the gifts she received from the marriage (see the wisdom of Jessie in chapter 8) are two truly beautiful teenage daughters.

Terri and her daughters live in suburban Philadelphia with Ned, their large turtle, Sandy (a.k.a. Fat Cat) who is their diabetic cat, Princess Kayley, the always neurotic and hissing feline, and their tick-collecting dog, happy, hairy Harry. Unfortunately, their black, bulging-eyed fish named Jorge (pronounced Hoar-hay or is it Hey- whore?) never made it to the pond on the Maguire estate. God rest his little soul. He is recently departed.

Join the Wives' Club

If your marriage story and your marriage advice are compelling and could benefit or inspire other wives, please consider participating in the next edition of *So This Is How It Feels to Be a Wife: The Next Dozen*.

Send us a one-page letter stating why you should be included, or complete the form on our Web site www.sothisishowitfeels.com. If selected, your life story will be in the next book in this series and you will become an honorary member of the Wives' Club.

We really look forward to hearing from you. Your story could change the life of another wife.

Thank you.

Send your one page letter to

So This Is How It Feels to Be a Wife

P.O. Box 1382

Southeastern, PA 19397